Samuel Rawson Gardiner

Letters relating to the Mission of Sir Thomas Roe to Gustavus Adolphus

1629-30

Samuel Rawson Gardiner

Letters relating to the Mission of Sir Thomas Roe to Gustavus Adolphus
1629-30

ISBN/EAN: 9783337228873

Printed in Europe, USA, Canada, Australia, Japan

Cover: Foto ©ninafisch / pixelio.de

More available books at **www.hansebooks.com**

LETTERS

RELATING TO THE MISSION OF

SIR THOMAS ROE

TO

GUSTAVUS ADOLPHUS.

1629—30.

EDITED BY

SAMUEL RAWSON GARDINER,

DIRECTOR OF THE CAMDEN SOCIETY.

PRINTED FOR THE CAMDEN SOCIETY.
M.DCCC.LXXV.

PREFACE.

Gustavus Adolphus is a hero of every nation, and it is unnecessary to apologise for the publication of a series of papers which bring him before us as painted by a writer so observant and intelligent as Sir Thomas Roe. The two papers added in the Appendix complete the portrait by strokes from his own hand. I have so recently given an account of the negotiation out of which they sprung that it would be needless to repeat here what I have said elsewhere. But even if these two papers stood alone they would be sufficient to establish the greatness of Gustavus's character. Their weight, firmness, and circumspection stand out in bold relief if they are contrasted with the diplomacy of James and Charles; but I should fancy that they hardly need that foil to attract the attention which they deserve.

A secondary interest attaches to Roe's mission as bringing before us the persistence with which Charles continued to interfere diplomatically on the Continent after all chance of interfering successfully was at an end. Yet, after all, Roe had to complain (p. 83) that in six months he had had no "letter, order, nor answer, nor money." Gustavus would not so have treated his ambassadors.

SIR THOMAS ROE'S MISSION TO GUSTAVUS ADOLPHUS.

To ordinary minds the winter of 1628-9 would have appeared a most unsuitable time for any warlike designs on the part of the King of England. The surrender of Rochelle in the previous autumn had been the crowning disaster of a long series of failures, and the domestic troubles had risen to such a height that no prudent man would have run the risk of entering upon diplomatic action which might possibly draw him into a war, which, in default of supplies from Parliament, could only end in disgrace and failure. But Charles had at least one quality in common with the nation over which he ruled. He never knew when he was beaten, and we find him in the years which followed the assassination of Buckingham as ready to interfere on the Continent diplomatically as he had been ready to interfere by force of arms whilst his favourite minister was alive.

In this course of action he had by his side till February 1632 the new Secretary of State, Viscount Dorchester, who, as Sir Dudley Carleton, had spent many years of his life as an ambassador at Venice and the Hague, and in two special missions to the court of France. He had thus acquired a considerable knowledge of continental affairs, and from his residence at the Hague and his intimate relations there with the exiled Elizabeth and her husband, as well as from his own bent of character, he had always taken a strong Protestant and anti-Spanish view of the questions at issue. But his absence from England dated from the autumn of 1610, before that winter session which marked the first open breach between the King and the Lower House; and, except for two brief intervals, he did not see his own country again till the spring of 1626, when he found himself suddenly called upon to answer for the Government in the House of Commons, then bent upon impeaching Buckingham. The opposition in Parliament and the nation therefore struck him as something not merely unreasonable but even unintelligible, and he would naturally be of opinion that a decided move in the defence of Protestant interests in Germany would strengthen the Crown in the eyes of Charles's subjects.

Very similar was the position of Sir Thomas Roe. He too had been long absent from England, from 1614 to 1621 in India; from 1621 to 1628 at Constantinople. Though he was geographically further removed than Carleton had been from the centre of European interests, he had by no means stood aloof from the great question of the day. Bethlen Gabor was one of the pieces in the game, and Bethlen Gabor might, it was hoped, be moved in this or that direction if Roe could induce the Sultan to pull the wires. Roe kept up a brisk correspondence with Elizabeth, sent her long letters of news, and received in return not a few of those short, playful epistles with which she knew how to keep up the good will of her friends, and in which she was accustomed to address them by some nickname of her choosing, Roe's special *soubriquet* being " Honest Tom."

Roe landed at Leghorn on August 26th, 1628,[a] on his way home from Constantinople. Travelling leisurely across the continent, he fell in with Carlisle,[b] who was coming back from Turin with the notion, that, as Spain and France were coming to blows in Italy, the Palatinate might perhaps be recovered with Spanish aid, thus renewing in 1628 the policy which had failed in 1622. Roe was not likely to share these opinions. He made his way to the Hague before returning home : there he seems to have remained for some time. He had brought a scheme of his own from Constantinople, and with or without the knowledge of the Government at home he made his proposals on the 27th of December to the Prince of Orange, that Frederick Henry who was to do so much for the advancement of his country's power. No name is attached to the following paper, but, as it is in Roe's handwriting, it may safely be attributed to him, especially as there is a reference in the document next following to a statement made by the Prince, which may very well have been an answer to this memorial.

I. *Memoir given by Sir T. Roe to the Prince of Orange.*

State Papers,
Holland.
Dec. 27
Jan. 6
1628-9.

The loss of the free trade of the Balticque sea is more dangerous to the kingdome of England and to the United Provinces then any other prosperity of the house of Austria, being the Indyes of the materialls of shipping, and, consequently, both of their strength, riches, and subsistence. There is no counsell so necessarye and so pressive as the consideration of meanes to preserve it in libertye, which being subjected to the Emperor, the Hans townes must of necessitye submitt to him.

There is no other consideration so forceable to draw those free cittyes to hope of libertye. and to joyne their forces with those who

[a] Roe's Negotiations, p. 826.
[b] Grandison to Roe, December 10th, 1628. *S. P. Dom.* vol. cxxii. 33.

seeke to defend it, as a resolution well grounded and declared to prefer that cause before all other quarrells.

Ther is no way nor meanes so ready and powrfull to effect this, and consequently to give breathing to the afflicted parts of Germanye, as by uniting the Kyng of Sueweland and the Prince of Transilvania, to which they are both well inclined, when they shall see the same affection, and a constant established foundation of meanes to prosecute the warre to one poynt.

Of these truths I suppose no practised man will doubt; but rather in the difficultye of drawing that Kyng and Gabor into such an union, in respect of the war of the first with Poland and the late peace of the other with the Emperor.

To which I say, that their interests are as great as ours, though more remote; that the first desires a peace, which Gabor can help to give, and he, to recover his honor by renewing the war which he hath lost by a forced and false peace. To procure a peace betwixt the Kyngs of Suevland and Poland the authoritye of the Grand Signor of the Tartars and Gabor must be used, and wilbe of great effect.

Gabor hath playnly declared that if the Kyng of Sueveland may be established head of the war that he will joyne with him 25,000 horse upon the conditions for his part already contracted; of all this ther shalbe given both sufficient reason and demonstration, whensoever any doubt shalbe objected.

To initiate this business it is first desired that his Ma[tie] of England and the Lords the States doe lay the foundation by describing their quota, to which the Kyng of Denmarke will contribute, for the payment of 40,000 doll[ars] monthly to Gabor, *pro singulis mensibus, quibus militavit,* and to give assured assignation, and to make their meanes appeare to the Kyng of Sueveland and Gabor for the constant payment therof in Venice, and, though this summe seeme great, yet in effect it wilbe easye to furnish, for it cannot be required above 4 moneths, from July to the end of November, for the Prince of Transilvania cannot be longer in the field, and this duly satisfyed, or deposited intyrely in Venice, will give him satisfaction.

The peace he hath lately made is the first degree of his ruyne; he hath the same desires, ambitions, and feares, which first made him take armes. He hath lately provoked the Grand Signor, who is greaved in this point only by Gabor, to whom alwaies hath beene referred the resolution of peace or war, and in July last an offer made to him of 160 thousand men in his ayd if he saw the opportunitye, or continued to doubt the fayth of the Emperor in the ratification of the peace which, though it be now confirmed betweene the Grand [Signor] and the Emperor, hath so many corruptions in the bodye thereof that it cannot stand nor the Grand Signor rest secure in yt; the articles mutually agreed are not the same and the differences irreconcileable. Lastly, all the ministers of the Grand Signor know and confess their dishonor and disadvantage by this peace, to which they were constrayned to yield by the Asian war, wherein, having now some ease, they wilbe ready to review their accounts with the Emperor, and, having reconciled Gabor, he is able by his arts or by necessityc to engage the Turkes at his pleasure. If a resolution be taken to assure Gabor, it is desired that a speedy course may be used to propose this league, and the conditions and assurances, by an ambassage to the Kyng of Suevland and a post sent to Gabor to signifye the treatye, that his deputies may assist therein: least they both bee engaged in the war of Poland. It is desired by Gabor, that the Kyng of Sweveland may appeare in Silesia, to whom he will obey, and, making the territories of Austria the seate of the war, he offereth to spoyle all the countrye round about and to burne whatsoever is found without the walled townes as far as Bavaria, when he shalbe secured of his retrayet by the King, and to serve him with his horse in all other occasions.

In the meane tyme it is above all things necessarye to send a fleete into the Balticque Sea to prevent the irrecoverable loss of the Sound and to enhearten the Kyng of Denmarke.

Roe probably left the Hague for England about the end of February, 1629.[a] In March Sir Henry Vane arrived in the Netherlands on a special mission to inform the Prince of Orange and the titular King and Queen of Bohemia, that, though the negociation for peace with Spain was not so far advanced as that with France, "yet in general of making peace with us, restoring our brother-in-law and dear sister to their patrimonial estates, ceasing the prosecution of the war upon our uncle the King of Denmark, and comprising our friends and allies the States of the United Provinces, we have large and ample offers; and, since these things cannot be affected but by one of two ways, either by treaty with Spain or by a war undertaken by France, the small appearance of the latter requires a trial to be made of the former, though never so doubtful, this course being not only now, but at all times to be embraced, what heretofore did not succeed may, by the blessing of God, according to the change of affairs, and the present conjuncture, as it now stands, have better issue." In short, the Duke of Savoy had advertised Charles that he had but to treat with Spain to get his wishes carried out; and to this assurance Charles replied, that he would send a person of trust to Spain and receive one from Spain. Vane was to communicate this to the Prince of Orange and to ask for his concurrence.[b] At the same time the King of Denmark was informed that as soon as Parliament had granted supplies Charles would be ready to assist him against the Emperor.

Not long after Vane left England, Sir James Spens, the usual emissary between Gustavus and Charles, arrived in England, apparently bringing news of the intended invasion of Germany by the Swedish King: "I have spoken freely and largely with Sir James Spens," writes Roe, on March 22nd, "who hath confidently communicated with me his employment, and the heroic designs of his brave prince and master. I dare not venture to discover the particulars, for the danger of Dunkirk[c] and the honesty of his promise, till he hath audience of his Majesty, which is directed for Tuesday next. In general I thought it would be comfortable for your Majesty to know that he will propound the same things which I did at the Hague, and avow me in all I have done here; and his offers are such and so easy and so magnanimous that they are not to be refused, unless we resolve to lie down and only cry, 'God help us.' That King and the King of Denmark have spoken together, and are parted with a perfect understanding and friendship. He hath order here to raise speedily three regiments, and if he prosper in England I hope this is the year of Jubilee."[d]

In the meanwhile Vane, who had arrived at the Hague on March 16th, was proceeding with his negotiation. He found that the Prince of Orange was firmly set against negotiation with Spain.[e] On April 10th, Dorchester wrote to Vane that his Majesty persisted in thinking that it would be well to try to get good terms from

---

[a] Elizabeth to Roe, March 2nd, 1629. *S. P. Dom.* cxxxviii. 8.
[b] Vane's Instructions, February 1629. *S. P. Holland.*
[c] *i. e.* lest this letter be taken by the Dunkirk privateers.
[d] Roe to the titular Queen of Bohemia, March 22nd. *S. P. Germany.*
[e] Conference with the Prince of Orange, March 20th. *S. P. Holland*

Spain. But he had little trust in the Spaniard, and merely intended to hear what they had to say.[a] On the 25th Vane was ordered to return to England.[b]

The result of Spens's mission, however, seems to have been that Charles determined to send Roe to the North, and the following paper, probably prepared for Carlisle,[c] shows what Roe's ideas on the subject were. It must be remembered that it was not yet known in England that the dissolution of Parliament on March 10 had frightened Christian of Denmark into the acceptance of the peace of Lubeck.

II. *Memoir by Sir Thomas Roe.*

State Papers, Holland.
Rec. May 18, 1629.

If his Majestie in this employment have any purpose to encourage the Kings of Denmark and Sueveland to continue resolute in the maintenance of that little libertye left in Germanye, and by their help to keepe open the Baltique Sea, and the trades therein, seeing the Prince of Orange gave me authoritye to declare in the name of the States that they would willingly concurre in such a councell or league ; it is necessarye (in my opinion) to communicate at least with them, and to penetrate how farre they will in such a case oblige themselves ; for to proceed without them is a deviation from good correspondence, may occasion a jealousye or envie on their parts, to the hinderance of the good effects, or rayse a suspition in those Princes whom his Matie doth seeke to assure of some misintelligence betweene us.

It is very likely they will assist both by their power and creditt, which I am sorrye, but must confesse wee need, and will much advantage the negotiation, especially if they may be procured to send a commissioner, or to write their letters concurrent to their ministers resident with those princes.

The King of Sweden hath lately by Camerarius, and doth now demand the renewing of their league expired for the conservation of the Baltique sea, and doth propose some meanes to pay a third or fourth of his army, which he dessignes for Germany, principally to keepe his horse from disbanding and falling to the enemye, which

---

[a] Dorchester to Vane, April 10th. *S. P. Holland.*
[b] Arundel to Vane, April 28th. *Ibid.*
[c] The indorsement is in Boswell's hand, who was in Carlisle's service.

is at this instant in consultation and ready for resolution. So that it seemes the conjuncture doth invite his Matie to make himselfe head of the partye, that willingly would obey him.

It will honor his Matie among the States that he doth take into his care the patronage of the publicque cause, and will encourage them to subserve to him in that and all other his occasions. And it is very requisite (in my judgment) by some concurrence with them, and application to them, to rayse and redeeme a declined and decryed opinion of our proceedings, and treatyes or the neglect of them.

Without this purpose and way, simply to make a peace betweene Poland and Sweveland is a noble worke and becoming his Maties greatnes and goodnes of mynde, but hath a. narrow extent of dessigne, and doth not assure nor conclude necessarilye any benifitt to the good cause. For though it pretends the setting-free of the King of Sueveland it doth also enlarge the Pole, who is as much an Austrian as the other is opposite. And if nothing but a bare peace be propounded to the first, and no league, ayd, nor contribution toward his active dessignes in Germany, I may suppose he wilbe content to enjoye his peace, and take example *per aliena pericula*. And I thinke no man can convince me with reason why he should marry our quarrell for charitye and without a dower.

It is very probable that both the King of Poland may be awed to make peace, and the King of Swevia be induced to undertake the protection of the suppressed, by using and applying the meanes of Gabor rightly. And it is in effect no more then the joyning of two leagues in one, for alreadye his Matie, Denmarke, and the States are in one league, and the King of Sweveland and Holland in another, both to one end, though they worke dividedly and so lesse effectually.

By establishing this union, and encouraging the King of Sueveland, the King of Denmarke is actually and reallye supplyed, to whom, if some essentiall favour be not done, he must accord with the enemye, and so cutt off all the fruits of this negotiation in the halfeway.

It wilbe untymely to move this to the States of Holland upon returne, when they will have concluded apart with the King of Sueveland, and they will seeme to have beene neglected in the foundation and only taken in as accessaryes.

If his Matie doth intend nothing but the treaty of peace betweene those princes, yett it wilbe necessarye first to acquainte the King of Sueveland, least he be jealous that the care is not for him, but only for ourselves, or worse.

If his Matie resolve to communicate with the Hollanders, I will be ready for what concernes myselfe within ten dayes, and leave my trayne servants to come after to Amsterdam to ship there, if possible, to prevent occasion, and gaine the yeare.

In the peace to be obteyned between Poland and Sueveland, which will open the Easterne trades, it is necessary to sette a Residence in the dominions of both princes. Because our last mart at Elving was so far envied, that an Act of Parlament was made in Poland that no cloth should be vented in that kingdome unlesse it were first sealed at Danske, which must either be revoked by treatye or els another seale established there, which will induce the peace by the benifitt, and reconcile us a great partye and many friends.

In this treatie the content of the Marquaes of Brandeburgh must be considered, our merchants here consulted, and direct instructions given me to warrant every poynt.

If I have not for brevitye sufficiently expressed my selfe, I am readye to open these intimations, which I thinke absolutely necessarye, when his Majestie shall call me.

On the 14th of June Roe took leave of the King, and, in answer to a question, was told by Charles that nothing would be done about a treaty with Spain without the communication, counsel, and fit respect of his friends and allies and the former leagues made with them.[a] The form at least of his embassy was not after Roe's liking. He wished to have been off long ago, and feared that the winter would be down upon him in the Baltic before he could get his business over.

The papers which follow speak for themselves.

III. *Sir Thomas Roe to Viscount Dorchester.*

MY LORD,

My truncks and servants are gone: the ship at Margrett readye; and I am like a young hawke upon the branches ready to flye, but want my wings; the playne truth is, as if it were a sicknes incureable, we doe all things too late. I see my busines cutt up at the rootes by delay. I foresee myselfe shutt up with the ice in a winters journey, which will cost his Majestie unnecessarilye more money then I stay for: this is deare interest and good husbandrye. I have no more patience nor can hide my thoughts. If your lordship will not goe or send to my Lord Treasurer this day and signifye the Kings pleasure your other paynes is lost, for I must despayre of service or comfort in this employment. If this night I know no resolution, I purpose to-morrow to make my owne innocence appeare before my master; which your lordship may prevent, and what I may pull upon me, who am

State Papers, Holland. June (?) 1629.

Your Lordships faythfull servant,
THO. ROE.

[*Addressed*] To the Right Hon. my very good lord the Lord Viscount Dorchester.

---

[a] Note of Conversation. *S. P. Holland.*

IV. *Instructions for Sir Thomas Roe.*

State Papers, Poland.
June 22/12, 1629.

Charles R. Instructions for our trusty and welbeloved Sir Thomas Roe, knight, our Ambassador Extraordinary to the King of Poland, and other Princes, States, and Townes in the Easterne Parts.

1. There being nothing more proper to princes whome God hath placed in eminent power and authority then to procure by good offices peace and quiett in Christendome betwixt such as are in warre, and to defend by common counsell and force the common liberty against the injury of oppressors: for as much as at one and the self-same time and the self-same part of the world there is occasion presented on the one side and enforced on the other for both these ends by way of ambassage betwixt such princes, states, and townes as have interest both in this peace and warre: Wee, for the satisfaction we have in your fidelity, and the many good testimonyes you have given of your ability in negociating with remote princes, who, by reason of the separation of our dominions, require in that respect so much the more dexterity in valuing our reputation with them, have made choyce of you for this important employment.

2. And to begin first with that which is first in intention though last in execution; the two Kings of Poland and Swede, being in warre betwixt themselves upon ancient quarrels newly revived, after divers pacifications which wee by severall messages and letters have bene desired to accommodate by some fitt instrument who in our name should interpose betwixt them (after the good indeavours which have bene used, though hitherto without effect, in the name of our good friends and allyes the States of the United Provinces, by theyr ambassadors expresly employed for that purpose), wee would have you undertake this worke as that which, besides other good respects, for the opening of the trade of Dantzick and other ports adjoining which are shutt up by reason of that warre, is behovefull both to our owne subjects and those of the United Provinces, which have formerly much frequented that easterly trade.

3. As you shall therefore be provided of letters of credence to those two kings which are in warre, the magistrats of Dantzick and such eminent persons in Poland as have invited us to this interposition, so shall you have addresse in your passage to the States of the United Provinces, with whome wee would have you treate and take light how this business may be best effected.

4. In Poland you are to assist yourself by Gordon our agent, whome you shall find in that court or in the towne of Dantzick, and in Swede by one Sanderson, our subject, who hath long lived in those parts and is an usefull instrument; and when Sir James Spence shalbe returned thether, who is here ambassador with us for the King of Swede, wee would have you hold strict correspondence with him as a person well affected and of good power with that province.

5. The other busines of defence is of larger extent, and compriseth not onely the interests of the two kings before mentioned and the towne of Dantzick but our owne in abundant manner, and those likewise of all the princes, states, and townes which are adjacent eyther to the North Ocean or the Baltique Sea, for it hath bene long and well observed how such as have bene instruments of the Austrian greatness with ayme to the universall Monarchye, having by practise procured much power in Poland to the prejudice of the auncient liberty of that kingdome, have for many yeares had a dessigne to bring the free towne of Dantzick (which notwithstanding the tytle of freedome doth acknowledge the superiority of that crowne) into a totall subjection, and to gett other seaports upon the Baltique Sea to make equippage of shipping and turne such materialls as wee and our friends and allyes drawe for that purpose out of those parts to theyr owne use, and further to intercept the transport of corne from Dantzick and those parts adjoyning which were wont to serve as a granary to the Low Countreyes and to our kingdomes likewise in tymes of scarcity.

6. This great dessigne marvelously to our prejudice and our friends likewise hath bene of late dayes so much advanced by other

accidents that not onely that trade is stopt to us but shipps of warre in a considerable number have bene furnished out of Dantzick to the assistance of the Austrian princes, who having gayned divers ports upon the Baltique Sea, 3 in Meckleburgh and 4 in Pomerania, and left nothing in effect unconquered upon that coast but Stralsondt, which is under the King of Swedes protection, are masters of all Holsteyn and Jutland except Luckstat onely, which countreyes opening many havens towards the ocean, the Spanyards doe there joyne in dessigne with the Imperialists, and by employing divers persons, some of quality and comaund, others of insight and experience in sea affayres, seeke to make a connection and correspondence betwixt the ports of those provinces and those they have in Flanders, after the same manner of Admirantasgos as they have established of late yeares betwixt the ports of Flanders and those of Spayne, and this with a great and dangerous dessigne of perfecting that dominion at sea which of late yeares beyond example of all former tymes they have advanced at land.

7. This is sett downe unto you the more at large because it may serve you as a ground and foundation on which to build your treaty of defence of the common liberty, which is your principall worke. And, because advice in such cases is commonly fruictles without example, wee doe now sett out a good squadron of our owne shipps victualled for 6 monthes under the conduct of Captayne Pennington, an experienced commander, with commission and instruction to repayre first into the Elbe, there to joyne with such shipps he shall find belonging to our deare uncle the King of Denmark[a] and our good friends the States of the United Provinces, and in that river and the seas adjoyning to employ himself as usefully as he possibly may for assistance of our friends and damage of our ennemyes; he being further charged to hinder, as much as in him lyeth, the transport of provision of victualls or munition of warre from those parts into the King of Spaynes dominions.

[a] The treaty of Lûbeck between the Emperor and the King of Denmark had been signed May $\frac{12}{22}$.

8. Wee doe further hold in our entertaynment a regiment of good men under experienced captaynes, commaunded by Generall Morgan, who being now employed by the King of Denmarke in an action of moment, wee have given Pennington speciall charge to assist and second him, and by such direction he shall receave from our ambassador with the King of Denmark, Sir Robert Anstrudder, or from the King himself, advance the service as he possibly may.

9. Now to take your further direction as your jorney lyes: you are to pass first into Holland, and there, having saluted the States in our name and delivered our letters of credence, to desire of them (after the accustomed manner of negotiation in that place) some deputyes to treate with you; and, having consulted of the two precedent points, one, the best meanes of effecting a peace betwixt the two Kings of Poland and Swede, for the reason before alleadged of freedome of comerce; the other, the defence of the Baltique Sea and the North Ocean, and knowne what they will contribute to both, wee would have you goe to the Prince of Orange and such of the States as are with him at the camp to treate with them to the same effect; and, having communicated to our deare sister and brother-in-lawe the effect of your ambassage, as well there as in other parts, you are (without longer stay than is necessary for receaving an answeare of the States, leaving the pursute of any thing which requires tyme of dispatch to our agent, Dudley Carleton, who is there resident with them) to take your jorney to our deare uncle the King of Denmarke with the best expedition you may.

10. With him, after delivery of your letters of credence with fitt complements, you are to hold the like language as with the States for the common service in these two precedent points; but there is a further occasion concerning us in particular, which requires great care and circumspection in the conduct thereof.

11. So it is that upon the pursute of the unhappy warre in Germany, wherein our brother-in-lawe and deare sister were violently and unjustly thrust out of theyr patrimoniall dignityes and estates, the conquest of the Imperialists, like a gangrene in a dying

body, passing from the Palatinat to Hessen, so further to the Princes of Neyther Saxe Creys (of which circle the King of Denmarke was generall), our father of blessed memory, foreseeing in his great wisedome the progresse of this mischiefe, not likely to stay any where at land or sea unles it were stopt by force, used indeavour by our ambassador, Sir Robert Anstruther, to persuade that King to declare and engage himself in that warre, with promise of assistance.

12. Many excuses being made and opportunityes lost whilst there was yet some remainder of strength in Germany to entertayne the ennemy, at length that king, growing sencible of his owne danger, in particular with ruyne of the publike, entred into conditions with Sir Robert Anstruther for the furnishing of a certayne number of men, horse, and foote, or a valuable proportion of money for theyr entertaynment; which he accepting in the King our father's name, and the King of Denmarke therupon taking armes, there was money furnished to a considerable sume by the King our father, and after his decease we continued that assistance partly in money and partly in ayde of men: wee sent in fower regiments under the commaund of Sir Charles Morgan, and of shipping conducted by Sir Sackville Trevor all to the uttermost possibility of our meanes, but chiefly by diversion, sending to that effect a royall fleete against the Spaniard in an enterprise upon Cales, which was performed in the name of our brother-in-lawe and deare sister as a German quarrell, in revenge of the invasion was made by the Spaniard upon the Palatinat.

13. This fleete in returne[a] lighting upon certayne French shipps laden with Spanish goods, and seising them by the right of warre, that seisure being taken in France (though very unjustly and contrary to the treatyes betwixt the two crownes) as a subject of counterseisure of English goods and marchandize in that kingdome, and one accident of offence begetting another, wherupon ensued a warre with that crowne likewise. This deprived us of such meanes

[a] This took place before it sailed. The whole story as told here is most unsatisfactory.

wee would most willingly have contributed to the King of Denmarke; yet upon the whole account of moneyes sent over by Sir Robert Anstruther, others furnished to the Denmarke Ambassadors, some taken up as pawnes, much spent in entertaynment of Generall Morgan's troopes, and somwhat furnished to officers which made leavyes in Scotland, with other disbursements, there hath bene furnished from hence *viis et modis* directly to that warre (besides the vast summes spent by way of diversion of the Spanish warre and the French, which fell in consequence thereof) above 300,000*l*.

14. This we doe not mention by way of discharge, as that wee had fully and totally acquitted ourselves to our deare uncle; but princes so nearely allyed in blood and conjoyned in interest of state are to complye one with another, and, measuring aydes by possibilityes, be sencible each of others condition, and wee need not conceale to a prince so neare us that whereof all the world doth take knowledge, that wee have had our incommodityes at home by the sinister practise of some disaffected subjects, much to the prejudice of our revenue, which wee are in a fayre way to overcome, and therby be the better enabled to assist our friends abroade.

15. Wee may well imagine, and wee have bene so informed, that our deare uncle hath mett with the like inconveniences amongst his subjects, and therunto wee ascribe the want in his army of the numbers of men and necessaryes of warre he made account of and stipulated with his confederates when he entred into armes; the difficulty he made in all treatyes and publique acts to mention the restitution of the Palatinat, which his ministers would never doe, though that were the originall and is indeed the permanent ground of our quarrell with the princes of the house of Austria; and, finally, the refusall of the ratification of the treaty of the Hagh (about which wee employed the Duke of Buckingham and the Earle of Holland in the yeare 1625), unles it were that certayne secret articles which were concluded at the same tyme (wherby our intention was explaned) might remayne unratifyed, which wee could no wayes admitt.

16. This we alleadge not by way of complaint nor for any further

purpose, but for your understanding, to the end that, knowing particularly how things have passed, you may be the better armed with answeares upon occasions, and to this purpose you shall have a writing with you which deduceth the state of these pretended debts and treatyes (specially this of the Hagh, which the ratifications thereof presented on our part totally but defectively on that Kings and the States likewise) more in particular; and you shall have in like manner a proposition made by the Lorde Rosencrantz, that King's last ambassador here with us in December last past, and answeared upon our order by our Commissioners for forrayne affayres in January following, which will give you some further light of that King's demaunds, and how far wee are able to goe for his satisfaction. You are now upon the whole matter so to conduct yourself and your negotiation with that King as, on the one side, not to dishearten him in despayre of our succors, which wee intend unto him to the uttermost of our possibility; and, on the other, to make the King our father's and our engagements otherwise understood then it seemes they are by such assignations he continueth to make over hether upon our Exchequer, as yf a franke and friendly supplye which hath bene heretofore furnished (and shall, God willing, be continued to the best of our ability) were a due debt.[a]

17. One debt wee acknowledge, and the interest thereof, as you will find by the answeare to the Danish ambassador; the other wee neyther doe nor will take upon us; but you are to handle the disavowing thereof cautiously, not to distast that King, nor to suffer the opinion of that engagement to rest upon us.

18. Wee have it advertised, both from our ambassador, Sir Robert Anstruther, and severall other wayes, that there is a treaty of peace very far advanced at Lubeck betwixt certayne Imperiall and Danish Commissioners, and that our deare uncle the King of Denmarke is in danger to be caryed much to his disadvantage (by the interests and feares of his Danish subjects and against his owne princely disposition) to a very prejudiciall peace both to himself

---

[a] *i. e.* Charles owns as a debt the money lent to his father, not the 30,000*l.* a month which he engaged to pay under the treaty of the Hague.

and his friends and allyes, and, yf you find that peace unconcluded, you may then represent unto him the present change of affayres of Europe, much more to his advantage then of late when the whole burthen of the warre lay upon his neck; a great part of the Imperiall forces being marched towards Italy to the number (as the latest advertisements beare) of 30,000 men, some drawne downe towards the Low Countryes in assistance of the Spanyard against the States' army, which is now in the field more powerfull than ever; others employed about Strasbourg with an eye to the French frontier, upon jealousy of that nation now our peace is made with that Crowne, wherunto, being persuaded by our deare uncle, wee much the more willingly hearkened, to the end that, being freed of that diversion, wee might give him the better assistance, and the French King likewise ayde him according to many promises, which wee are glad to heare doe already begin to be putt in effect by some moneyes newly sent by an expresse minister out of France, persuading that King, the same way as wee have reason to doe, not to make peace dishonorably or disadvantagiously.

19. But, yf you find the peace shutt up and concluded, wee would have you then require a copie of the articles, to the end wee may see how far and in what manner wee are interested, and in all event for satisfaction of our marchants (a people ever subject to feares and jealousyes), not for any distrust wee have of our deare uncle. You are to procure good assurance that in the passage of the Sondt no stopping or seizure shal be made of theyr shipps and goods by way of arrest for satisfaction of pretended debts. And this is the effect of your particular nogotiation in that court, which, though it hath a mixture with the publike as it concernes peace or warre, yet are you to observe how it doth chiefly reflect upon our interest and our subjects to deliver us from undue pretentions and them from unjust seisures.

20. In your jorney further, whether you will begin with Poland or Swedeland wee must leave to your discretion, according to such light you shall gather in Holland and in the King of Denmark's

court, most effectually to advance our affayres; but wee heare the failing of the States' interposition for a peace betwixt those two Kings proceeded in part [from]*a* theyr having made theyr addresse to Swede, which by the haughty humor of the Pole was taken in disdayne, and, wheresoever you doe begin, the conduct of this busines must more depend upon [your]*b* owne iudgement then upon direction; this being our chiefe ayme in the pacification of those two Kings to open and secure commerce after the ancient manner of treatyes with those Crownes and the townes of Dantzick and Elbing, according as the change of affayres upon the successe of that warre and the pacification you are now to treate will permitt.

21. But this state of affayres of the kingdome of Poland having long rested in these termes, that the King and his personall dependants being governed by the Jesuites, and by them, as active instruments of the Austrian greatnes, alwayes caryed to the advancement of that house, and the chiefe nobility and gentrye of that kingdome remayning opposite to that Jesuiticall faction as maintayners of the ancient libertyes and freedome of that countrey, which they alwayes make appeare in theyr assemblyes when they conveanc together by way of Parliament, shewing a good inclination to the profession of our religion, at least to the maintenance of freedome of conscience which the lawes and constitutions of that countrey doe allowe,—you are in your addresses to have especiall regards of such of the nobility as stand that way affected, and in your proceeding in the peace you are specially to have regard to the conditions thereof, that yf they tend by the practise of the Jesuites and theyr partye to the concluding with the King of Swede and withdrawing his assistance from the King of Denmarke or from restoring the liberty of Germany, which he is entered into with so princely a resolution notwithstanding his other engagements by the defence of Stralsondt,—in this case wee, preserving publike respects of state before our particular interests of marchandise, doe not thinke it fitt your endeavors should tend to the advancement of that peace;

a " for " in MS. *b* " our " in MS.

but otherwise, yf the King of Swede be left free to pursue what he hath so royally undertaken, wee would then have you goe on in the pacification between those two Crownes according to our first intention.

22. There is a due debt of moneyes lent by the King our father to the King of Poland to the value of 10,000*l*., the documents and instruments whereof you shall have with you, or at least authenticall copyes of them, to recover it for us, as wee cannot but confesse wee have neede. And, touching the opinions of the easterne trade, wee esteeme it necessary to settle a residence in the dominions of both those Kings (the Pole and Swede), because wee have it informed that our last mart at Elbing was so far envyed that an Act of Parliament was made in Poland that no cloth should be vented in that kingdome unles it were first sealed at Dantzick, which must eyther be revoked by treaty or else another seale established there. This may prove a good inducement to the peace by the benefitt thereof, and gayne unto us many friends.

23. In this treaty the interest of the Marquis of Brandenburgh is to be considered, who hath written unto us that he will assist in it by his deputyes, and before your departure our marchants are to be consulted with how best to advance theyr affayres; and you may promise in our name to the subjects of both those princes and townes free trade, with theyr wonted good treatment, in these our dominions; and yf you find it objected that theyr shipps are som. tymes intercepted in these seas, such as trade into Spayne, you shall require them to understand this rightly, that it is onely to impeache the transport of equippage of shipping and munition of warre into that King's dominion, without the helpe whereof wee are sure that King could not so much trouble the state of Christendome, and whilst wee continue in warre with him this prohibition is agreable to all lawes, naturall, nationall, and civill.

24. There is a Prince in those parts, the Duke of Curland, with whome wee have allyance and particular friendship, in whose favor wee would have you employ yourself according to such informations

he will give you; and you are to have your aspect further into Transylvania, it being very probable that both the King of Poland may be awed to make a peace and the King of Swedeland induced to undertake the protection of the suppressed, by using and applying the meanes of Gabor rightly; and it is in effect a joyning and linking of three leagues in one;·there being one betwixt us and the United Provinces for restitution of the Palatinat and mutuall defence, into which the King of Denmarke came by the treaty of the Hagh as accessory; another betwixt the King of Swede and the States for the freedome of the Baltique Sea, about which the Kings of Denmarke and Swede, at theyr late interviewe, did likewise contract an allyance; a thyrd, betwixt the King of Swede and Gabor, who having mett together in mariage in the same house[a] have established betwixt themselves a particular intelligence.

25. All these being to one and the self-same end, though they worke dividedly, yet it may be in one regard more effectually, because, amongst many confederats in one body, by reason of remotenes of place and severall interests, there can seldome fall out a right understanding. You are therefore to use an active industrye to make all these princes co-operate towards the common defence by way of intelligence, since wee find that cannot be which hath bene many tymes heretofore proposed, and now lastly by Sir James Spence, as Ambassador from the King of Swede, by way of union and confederation, wherunto you may make knowne unto that King when you come to his presence, as likewise unto such others as wish well unto it, wee are so far from being adverse, that as the King our father did declare his good liking of it wee should embrace it most willingly; but in this conjuncture of affayres it is more behoovefull, according to former agreements, wee should employ ourselves to the same end, though in severall parts, by present action, then entertayne the tyme in negotiation. It rests onely for your instruction that you take with you such treatyes as have formerly passed betwixt us and such princes, states, and townes you

[a] They married sisters of the Elector of Brandenburg.

are to deale with: wherewith our Secretary shall have commaund to furnish you; and, for such further circumstances as in a charge consisting of so many parts with princes so remote cannot so well be prescribed unto you, you are to take counsell of tyme and place and present occurrences and governe yourself by discretion; advertising from tyme to tyme as you find commodity of sending, and according to the importance of occasions, by expresse messengers, in what state you find affayres where you goe, to the end that in such things as may attend tyme of answeare you may receave our further order.

In all places, at your first publique audiences, our pleasure is you should speake by interpretors; at other tymes wee leave it to your liberty.

DORCHESTER.

Greenwich, this 20th of June, 1629.

V. Sir Thos. Roe's Speech at his "First Audience to the States General, by Interpreter."

MY LORDS,

His Matie my Lord and Master having taken into his Royall consideration the present estate of the troubles and desolations in Germany, and having resolved to apply such means as God hath given him, and as in his wisedome he hath thought conduceable to the publicque interest, hath commanded me to visitt and salute them in his name as his good friends and confederates, and to assure you of his constant purpose by effects in all your occasions on his part to nourish this confidence betweene his Matie and your Estates; to which purpose he hath thought necessarye to that good correspondence he doth and will hold with you, to communicate freely his intentions, and on them to take your advise and counsell, well-assured of your concurrence in all endeavours for the common cause; and for your better assurance he hath commanded me to deliver unto your Lordships this his letter, to which you may be pleased to

State Papers, Holland. July $\frac{2}{12}$, 1629.

be further referred. And because you know the prejudice of lost tyme I will be bold to entreat you to appoint some Commissioners to heare and to consult with me with such convenient speed as may fitt your great affayres and my hast. Lastly, I shall desire of you to beleeve of me, however, in other essentiall respects, the most unworthy of the honor of this function, yet that never man came hither with more honest and zealous affection to the publicque nor your Lordships' particular service.

VI. *Roe's proposition to the States General.*

State Papers, Holland.
July $\frac{5}{15}$, 1629.

Abbregé de la proposition du Chevalier Roe, Ambass^r Extroad^{re} de sa Ma^{te} de la Grande Bretagne, faicte aux Deputés des Seigneurs Estats Généraux des Provinces Unies, le $\frac{3}{15}$ Juillet, 1629.

Sa Ma^{te} mon Seigneur et Maitre ayant sagement preveu le danger imminent de la liberté de la Mer Baltique, et senti la perte que l'interruption du traffic dicelle apporte, occasionés par la guerre entre les Rois de Pologne et de Suede, et qu'il y a apparence que les forces Imperialles seront attirées dans la Prussie à l'oppression du Roy de Suede et assujettissement de cette Province à la maison d'Austriche estant aussi requise par le Roy de Pologne de s'entremettre comme Médiateur de paix à laquelle le Roy de Suede s'est declaré n'estre pas contraire, il lui a pleu m'imposer la charge de moyenner entre ces deux couronnes.

Les raisons qui ont induit sa Ma^{te} à s'interposer en cest affairse (qui de soy mesme est un office convenable à un Roy Chrestien) sont deux :

1. La necessaire consideration de l'ouverture du traffic de la cité de Dansick et autres villes libres, pour le proffitt de ses propres subjets et des Provinces Unies, ce qui estant assés evident n'a besoing d'amplification plus large. A cecy appartient un soing particulier, que l'on doit avoir de la ville de Dansick, qui autrement pourra facilement estre opprimée en sa liberté ou par l'Empereur ou par le Roy de Pologne.

2. La seconde raison est la consideration du danger commun et de la defense de la Mer Baltique; le premier n'est que trop manifeste, à raison de l'accroissement de la puissance de l'Empereur en ces quartiers là, ayant à sa devotion et subjection tant de Ports en Meckelburg et Pomeranie et puis que Wallestein a receu l'investiture de l'une et que sur l'autre ne manqueront poynt des pretensions semblables, après la mort du Duc Regnant. Que si ces pays viennent une fois à estre absoluement reduits à la volonté et obeissance de la maison d'Austriche, tous les Princes et villes Hansiatiques sur ceste mer seront par la necessité du traffic peu à peu et comme insensiblement subjuguées et contrainctes de recevoir la loy de l'Empereur specialement iceluy estant en paix et amitié (comme l'on pretend) avec le Roy de Dannemarc qui a le pouvoir seul d'ouvrir et de fermer ceste mer, à qui il lui plait. Sur ces considerations sa Ma^{te} m'a commandé de communiquer franchement et en confiance à vos Seigneuries ses desseins et par quelles voyes elle veut procéder, et en cela demander vostre conseil et advis, et vous requerir de joindre avec elle pour l'accomplissement de ces deux fins, assavoir l'ouverture du traffic et la defense commune, et de vous assurer que l'interest de vos Seigneuries comme de ses bons amis et alliés, qui est aussi cher et autant prevalable au soing qu'elle porte du public que le sien propre, ou celui de ses propres sujets.

Quant au premier, la liberté du traffic, sa Ma^{te} estime que le propre et naturel remede est d'appaiser les differens entre ces deux Rois estant deux choses incompatibles que la guerre et le traffic. Pourveu que la paix se puisse faire à telles conditions que le Roy de Suede demeure en liberté de proceder en ses resolutions heroiques pour la defense de ces provinces, villes, et mers, et qu'il ne soit diverti de ses nobles et genereux desseins. En quoy sa Ma^{te} desire aussi l'advis de vos Seigneuries, et qu'il vous plaise me communiquer vostre opinion avec tels conseils qui puissent faciliter la perfection de ceste œuvre.

Pour le second ass[urer?] la defense commune, sa Ma^{te} croit et tient qu'il n'y a poynt de moyens plus prompts ni plus puissants que de cherir et encourager le Roy de Suede, Prince de grande prudence et valeur, et heureux en ses entreprises. Et pour ce qu'il est à craindre qui, suivant l'example des autres par un soing de soy mesme trop precipité, il ne vienne à delaisser le public estant à soupçonner que l'Empereur lui offrira des conditions assés flatteuses ou cherchera sa ruine totale par armes, sa Ma^{te} m'a donné instruction, après que j'aurai premièrement preparé les choses requises à un tel traitté avec le Roy de Danemarc, d'assurer le Roy de Suede que sa Ma^{te} est resolue de correspondre avec lui et de lui donner toute aide qui sera jugée possible et expediente, et de l'animer à continuer ses braves desseins avec constance, jusques à ce que l'on puisse meurement considerer par quels moyens, et en quelle mesure, on le pourra secourir. En quoy, quand sa Ma^{te} sera pleinement et vrayement informée des intensions de ce Roy et de ses moyens et manquements et que c'est qu'il demandera, et attendra de ses amis et alliés, elle donnera ordre pour pleine asseurance et satisfaction d'icelui laquelle ne se peut pour le present determiner ni conclurre en esgard à l'estat present de Danemarc et au peu de conoissance que nous avons encore des articles de ceste paix, et qu'il n'y a poynt eu d'ouverture specialle faicte de la part du Roy du Suede.

Sur ce poinct Sa Ma^{te} m'a pareillement commandé de demander le conseil de vos Seigneuries, et de vous persuader jusques là de vous declarer pour l'encouragement et confirmation du dit Roy de Suede, affin que je lui puisse apporter de votre part le soulagement de vos resolutions de contribuer en telle mesure qu'il sera convenable, et que par la bonne aide et assistance de vos Seigneuries je soye rendu capable de commencer une negotitiation[a] avec ce Roy pour la defense publique. En quoi sa Ma^{te} fera tout ce qui appartient à un Roy de telle puissance et zele à la cause commune. Finalement qu'il vous plaise aussi m'aider avec vos lettres et memoires vers ces Princes et villes libres interessées en ces affaires et en la cause du commun, pour l'accomplissement des desirs de sa Ma^{te} et de vos Seigneuries.

[*Indorsed*] Proposition faicte et donnée aux Deputés des Estats Generaux des Provinces Unies le $\frac{3}{13}$ Juliet, 1629.

Their deputies were 6 :
    Monsr FINCK of Gelderland.
    Monsr BOCKHORST of Holland.
    Monsr BEAUMONT of Zeland.
    Monsr RODA of Utrecht.
    Monsr LUCTEREN of Zutphen.
    Monsr TER-COULEN of Over-Issell.

VII. *Answer given to Sir Thomas Roe.*

They withdrew themselves to consult together, and Mons. Finck of Gelderland, in the name of the rest, giving his Matie humble thanks for his favour to them and care of the publique, required the substance of my discourse and proposition in writing, which I promised. [State Papers, Holland. July $\frac{3}{13}$, 1629.]

To that part wherein I desired to know their opinion in generall of the peace between the two Crownes of Suede and Poland, and to be informed by them of the difficulties their Ambassadors found in that negotiation, that I might the better direct my selfe, and that they would be pleased to contribute to mee their counsells, assistance, and memorialls for the accomplishment of that treaty, they answered, that they did approve and concurre with his Matie in the desire of that peace, and would expresse it upon consultation, having then only order to heare and relate.

For the other, they referred mee to Mons. Beaumont, who had bin one of their ambassadors employed to that effect, who freely declared the first difficulty did arise from a refusall of the King of Poland to acknowlege the King of Suede for king, and to renounce his pretensions upon that crowne. The second upon restitution of the places taken by the King of Suede in Livonia and Prussia, upon which the nobility of Poland insisted, and which the King of

Suede was willing to surrender upon payment of his charge of the warre, which mony could not be found. Lastly, that he found as much power as aversnes in the cleargy and Jesuites, who wholly opposed the treaty. He thought the making of a peace would be difficult, and not so advantageous to the King of Suede as a long truce, whereby he might hold possession of some seaports as cautions, and to this counsell he applied himselfe.

VIII. *Conference between Sir Thomas Roe and the Count of Schwarzenberg.*

State Papers, Holland.
July $\frac{4}{14}$, 1629.

Conference with the Count of Swartzenburg,[a] 4 and 5 July, 1629.

He related the cause of the warre to arise from the King of Suede, who by often breach of promise cast the Elector of Brandeburgh into a jealousy of the King and State of Poland: so farre as they quarrelled his estate in Prussia as forfeited. I observed in all his discourse that he cast the blame upon the King of Suede.

I desired to know what were the difficulties that the Dutch Ambassadors fell upon in their treaty. He answered, that they landing in the Prussia of Brandeburgh were inticed by the Chancellor of Suede to speake first with him, and so fell into a jealousy of the King of Poland; and after removing and staying long at Dansick they grew worse suspected, as negotiating in that towne a neutrality for the King of Suede,—insomuch, that comming to court they scarse were admitted audience, as being partiall; but after they had obtained leave to treate they spent much time about the place, titles, and ceremonyes, but never entred into the substance. I asked what proposition he thought so indifferent and just as might be acceptable on both sides, to which he replied, absolute restitution of the King of Suede. I demanded whither it were safe for his master

[a] On behalf of the Emperor.

to advantage the Pole so much, seeing he confessed that they pretended a forfeiture, to which he replied, there was no other way of peace, for I should find the affaires changed; the King of Poland reconciled to a faction of his subjects; his eldest sonne assured of the succession and the forces of the Emperour in his ayd, which would make him high in his demands. In this I found him all imperiall; only he confessed that if by peace and restitution the King of Suede were not removed out of Prussia, that he thought it was the Emperor's purpose to sett up his owne pretenses to the wholle country and to oppresse the Elector, and by the King's consent to deceive the Poles, and to change the dependance *in feudo* of that province and to give it to Casimir, the second sonne, and that this he did beleeve was the secrett end of those auxiliars sent by the Baron Arnheim.

He councelled mee to land in a neutral part, intimating that of Brandeburgh, and to send a secretary to both Kings to signifie my arrivall, and to prepare a place of convention indifferent, wherin he knew the Elector's Commissioners should assist if he were not himselfe in person. He told mee the truce taken in expectation of his Maties mediation was ended the last of June, and that the Elector had procured a prolongation of six weeks, but that he feared the descent of the imperiall forces would bring all into confusion, being purposely interposed to prevent a treaty of peace, and that he now thought the Emperor would become a party both in the peace and warre.

[*This and No. 9 are indorsed*] Conference with the deputies of the States Generall the 3, and with Count Swartzenburg 4 and 5 July, 1629.

IX. *Sir Thomas Roe to Viscount Dorchester.*

My Lord,

I arrived at the mouth of the Mase on Munday night with Capt. Pennington's whole fleete, being embarqued on the Adventure. I

State Papers, Holland. July $\frac{4}{14}$, 1629.

mett the rest at sea, who I hope are returned safe to the Downes according to their order. On Tuesday I gott to Delfe, where Mr. Carleton mett me and received me as your Lordship's servant. The next day some of the States mett me according to custome and conducted me to their house, and entertayned me honestly. That night I asked audience, and the morning (Thursday) I went to the Court of the States Generall and delivered to them with his Maties letter a few words of ceremonye, of the generall of my imployment, and desired them to appoynt deputies to heare and consult with me with as much speed as their owne affayres and my hast would permitt. This I told by interpreter, and with the assistance and communication of your nephew. After a replye from them of due respect to his Matie and other complements, they desired that I would give them in writing what I had sayd, to which I replyed that they had the substance in his Maties letter, and that I thought it superfluous: when ther was any matter of deliberation propounded I would endeavour to give them requisite content. On Fryday they sent six deputies, for every province one, to Mr. Carleton's house, whither I desired to remove and now am, to his trouble, to whom I proposed the subject of my legation; and, they separating themselves to consult, required it of me in writing, which I could not refuse, unless that I would prejudice myselfe by suspition or singularitye, which, with the consent of your nephew, I have to-day presented to them. And, because they will not answere untill they have advised with the Prince of Orange to gayne tyme, I purpose to goe to him on Munday,[a] and thereby hope to advantage myself in the answere. This breefe account I thought fitt to give y^r Lordship that you may see I loose no tyme, and in generall to lett you know that I have not only proceeded in confidence with Mr. Carleton but by his approbation and advice, having acquainted him with my instructions and my sense of them, wherein I find that I have a worke of greater curiosity, to weigh wordes and to cutt by a thread then direct matter to build upon, though in generall I judge more

[a] 6 July.

might have been done here if I had had more scope. The negociations of Camerarius hangs in the bryars; the peace of Denmarke is diverslye understood here, but in the worst sense. Mr. Carleton will send your Lordship a breefe of the freshest advise from Sir Ro: Anstruther, and give you better relations of the leaguer and this State then you can expect from me. When I returne I shall have made observations to judge upon, and then I will trouble your Lordship with the coppies and particulars of my proceedings by journall, and hasten towards Denmarke. Of my deligence I beseech your Lordship to make relation to his Matie, wherein I shall need no other wings nor spurrs then the zeale of his service and the ease of a charge which I know not but as the satyre that kissed fire, and too heavy for my temporall foundation. I yet undergoe my burthen in confidence of a good master and in assurance of the extension of your favour and protection to

Your Lordship's humble devoted servant.

Haghe, $\frac{4}{14}$ July, 1629.

Returning from the armye I purpose but two dayes stay here.

[*Indorsed*] To my Lord of Dorchester, 4 July, 1629.

X. *Sir Thomas Roe's Conference with the Prince of Orange and the Deputies of the States Generall.*

On the 7 of July I arrived at Renen, where the King of Bohemia mett me, purposely come from the camp. I delivered his Maties letters to him and the Queen, and made a relation of my employment, applying it in the generall to the advantage of his Highnes and his affayres. He returned his Maties thanks, and seemed not only to concurre but to submit himselfe and his opinions wholy to his Maties direction, upon whose wisdome and goodnes he did entirely depend, but in matter of advise he showed a tendernes to declare, doubting that my message had not wings to beare up the

State Papers, Holland. July $\frac{18}{28}$, 1629.

weightie body of so great a dessigne as the encouragement or support of the King of Swede, who would (as he beleeved) hazard no more without realitye and assurance of sufficient and constant supplye.

9. The 9 day I wayted on the King of Bohemia, to the camp before Boisleduc, and arrived late, and was lodged by the Prince of Orange that night; I gave him his Maties letters and desired a conference with him in the morning.

10. Wherein I related the substance of my negotiation to the same purpose that I had spoken to the Deputyes of the States, and to the written propositions given them; I desired his advise and the ayd of his authority with them, to hasten me such an answere as might correspond with his Maties purposes and the generall good. I putt him in mynd of the power given me from him to assure his Matie of a readines in the States to concurre with him in any action that should take care of the libertye of the Balticque Sea or the safety of the King of Swede, which had beene an especiall motive of my passing by these parts both to communicate and to consult with his Excellencye and the Lords of these provinces to that effect.

His answere was, that he had yet received no particular from the States Generall, but of my arrivall; and, therefore, could not (by the rule he held in such affayres) propound busines first to them. To the matter it selfe he approved his Maties care of opening the trades in those seas and his counsell to that end to make peace betweene the Kings of Poland and Swede as the only way and remedye; he acknowledged the benefitt and almost the necessitye thereof to this State, which they had expressed publicquely, by sending their ambassadors to the same purpose; and therefore wished his Matie all honor and successe in so worthy and necessarye an office, which to particulars of the States he would recommend, and doubted not I should receive an answere of satisfaction. To the second poynt of the publicque defence, he sayd he was constant to what he had told me formerly, because he knew the States were constant to their owne and their friends' advantages, but that i became not them to declare first. They were, in effect, left alone in the warr: the Emperor, by the King of Denmark's peace, being sett loose upon them, so that they had enough to doe and more then they could continew to defend their owne libertye. Notwithstanding, if his Matie had beene pleased to declare his resolution, he was assured the States would not have beene wanting to doe what they were able; but how farr to that poynt they would answere at present he could not foresee, nor might persuade them with discretion to enter into particulars upon a generall discourse. He wished the support of the King of Swede as most necessarye, but seemed to decline all treaty of league that must constantly and determinatly bind (modestly reflecting upon our past treatyes), but rather intimated a way of voluntarye contribution, which yet he thought would not assure that king. In generall, with great gravitye, he made light of my proposition as being no way grounded. He did formalise upon Rubens' negotiation in England as verye unseasonable, to which I replyed that Sr Henry Vane would give a present account, and that I had no other order nor knowledge but that his Matie therein would send a just and right satisfaction to all his friends. I moved him particularly to procure the States to contribute so much encouragement as I might be able to assure the King of Swede in case of any league of the subsidy given to Denmarke; but he would promise nothing more then a generall recommendation of the same stuffe and temper that I brought him.

From him I went to the Deputies of the States Generall for the camp and did the like office. I found them verye sensible of the profitt of the treatye betweene the Kings of Pole and Swede, giving his Maties humble thanks for so particular a favour as the communication with them; to that poynt by Mons. Vosberghen they discoursed largely; he gave me many good and wise cautions and advertisements in the managing of the treatye, especially to take care of the King and to avoyd the rocke of Polish jealousye: to this part they promised to contribute their counsell to the States. To the second, the common defence, he insisted much upon the peace of the King of Denmarke, and spake doubtfully and fearefully of some secrett articles; he opened the envye of those nations Danish and Swede, and that any intimation of succour or supply that might give honor to the King of Swede would rather disturbe the King of Denmarke then winne upon him, and therefore wished me not to begin there; but from his owne articles with the Emperor, wherein is reserved an inclusion of his Matie and the States to ask what was his intention therein and what counsell he would give for their comprehension, and what wayes to convert that peace to their benefitt, thereby to discover his purposes toward them, and thereupon to proceed to assurance of their subjects' trades; which, being gayned to enlarge so far upon the common defence as might not invidiously cross the other, because he thought that King had neyther will nor power in respect of his counsell that over-ruled him in the peace, to doe much for the generall, and therefore that it was more safe to pass by it then to fayle or discover further intentions untill they were more assured; but that, as they desired above all things the quiett of that sea and the safetye of the King of Swede and the libertye of the Hans Townes, so they would write to the Lords the States their opinion to concurre with his Matie in all his royall purposes, declining utterly any other declaration.

11. I returned towards the Haghe with more satisfaction in that I had seene then what I had done, having gone round all the miraculous workes and visited all the approches to their points, and judged the towne crestfallen,[a] in want and despayre.

[*Indorsed*] Conference with the Prince of Orange and the Deputies of the States General at the Camp, 10 July, 1629.

[a] Bois-le-Duc., to which the Prince was then laying siege.

XI. *Sir Thomas Roe to Frederick, titular King of Bohemia.*

May it please your Matie,   State Papers,
  If I should leave this countrye without acknowledgement of   Holland.
your Maties virtues and favours, which I have abundantly seene and   July $\frac{14}{4}$, 1629.
tasted, the sinne of foule ingratitude would hang over and affright
me in all my journye. I am able to returne your Matie nothing,
and Kings expect nothing but good hearts from their servants.
Your Matie hath knowne what my master hath commanded me to
say and doe in this employment, wherein I find many difficultyes
and have little advanced here. The entrye of the Emperor's troopes
into Prussia, I feare, have a larger dessigne then the contemplation
of the peace of Poland, and I shall find now a third partie interessed
and the warre broke out, for we have certayne advice of a fight
betweene the King of Swede and Arneim; the successe I send your
Matie enclosed, as it comes from Lubecke; but Arnheim's letters
make it worse, though he confess the King did make an honorable
retraict. I will hasten my journye with all possible speede, hearing
by the English troopes of Colonell Morgan arrived at Enchusen;
that the King of Denmarke is in Holstein; and, as it is the intention
of his Matie to apply this negotiation particularly to your service,
and to the benefit of your affayres, so, if God prosper me, I will
endeavour by some effects to give your Matie testemonye of my
zeale therein, and how far your infinite favours have obliged me to
do you service. Of what I shall be able to do I will presume to
render your Matie assiduous account, and give me leave to beseech you
to ease us of the care and to prevent your owne danger: your Matie
ought not to tempt an all [a] accident. Almighty God keepe your
Matie safe and restore you to the dignitye of your meritts, and the
prayers of   Your Maties most humble servant.

Hagh, $\frac{14}{4}$ July, 1629.

[*Indorsed*] To the King of Bohemia, 14 July, 1629.

[a] *sic;* probably for ill.

XII. Sir Thomas Roe to Viscount Dorchester.

State Papers,
Holland.
July 14/24, 1629.

My Lord,

My letter of the 4 July hath given your Lordship account of my passage and entrance into my busines here. The enclosed will declare how I have since passed my tyme to this day at noone. My success hath not answered my diligence, finding this state full of care and trouble, having their hands full both of invasion and defence, and their heads of feare of the encrease of the enemies' forces by accession of the Imperialls. This hath hindered me both in tyme and the extent of their declaration, which what it wilbe two dayes will enable me to assure his Matie. In the meane tyme I thought necessarye so far to be provided as to send your Lordship all, which, if you thinke superflous, you may teach me to spare yow and myselfe. I fynd here that though these men are as sencible as can be expected of both poynts committed to my charge, as their present plantation in Muscovye doth strongly witnes, yet they pretend that the same generalityes have beene often propounded without effect, and so they less esteeme this. In clearer tearmes, they hope and believe little, and yet I am persuaded would doe much if I had power to trye them; but I am tyed to so strict a forme of proposition that I speake rather leafe gold then solid mettall. This freenes his Matie will pardon me, because I would have built strongly. I omitt to trouble your Lordship with more of this untill I see their answere, and will presume to conclude with my opinion of the present state of these provinces. It may be counted a paradoxe to thinke that theire prosperitye at Boisleduc will facilitate a peace, which I for many reasons beleeve, though others suppose they wilbe blowne up with insolence; but I consider they doe not dessigne great conquests, but a securetye, which this towne may give them; and the expence is so immense that they wilbe glad to take breath. Besides, the bold attempt of the enemy, almost desperate, to enter their countrye without a retraict doth amaze and teach them what fury and desperation may doe; so that, in my opinion, if they winne they wilbe content; if they loose they wilbe abject and the countrye discontent, and that conjuncture of a treatye for them very propitious. Your Lordship will find by a note within this letter that the King of Swede hath had a check, and that the Emperor is entered, not so much in contemplation of the peace for Poland, as a third party, so that my negotiation will find new difficultyes, and all sides perhaps exasperate, and the comforte that I shall carry only queres. Only his Maties name and authoritye doth strengthen me, whom I beseech by your Lordship's mediation to accept my endeavours, which shall be winged with diligence and fidelitye, and that yow wilbe pleased to continew me in your patronage as

Your Lordship's most humble devoted servant,
THO. ROE.

Haghe, $\frac{15}{25}$ July, 1629.

I have not stepped one foote nor uttered a sillable without the company and approbation of your nephew, who hath irreparrably obliged me.

All the publicque ministers here have visited me, only the French have taken no notice; perhaps he knows not his trade or is sorry for the peace, for I know him well by his negotiations at Vienna.

[*Indorsed by Dorchester*] From Sir Th. Roe the 15 of July, received at Theobald's by an expresse the 26, *stilo veteri*, 1629.

After some negociations in Denmark, Roe proceeded to the seat of war. His letters which follow give an account of his dealings with Gustavus.

XIII. *Sir Thomas Roe to Viscount Dorchester.*

MY LORD,

I arrived at Konigsberg the 18 Aug., where I was well received and used by the Prince Elector of Brandenberg, and from where I

State Papers,
Poland.
Sept. $\frac{7}{17}$, 1629.

instantly wrote with all due respect to the King of Swede. There I enformed myselfe of the estate of the affayres, how they stood, and by the conduct of his Commissioners, that were ready to goe to the treatye begun by an enterloping French ambassador, Mons. Charnassy, gott to the Polish camp (for there was no other way) the 23 day. The King and Prince being retired to Warsow, the next day I sent Mr. Gourdon to the Swedes' quarters, to advise the King that I was comming to him to offer my selfe to that dutye which his Matie had commanded me; but he refused me audience upon vayne quarrells for titles or epithites; and so I fell upon a dispute with him six dayes, which being accommodated, the 29 I came to his campe, with honorable reception, and had that night audience and delivered him his Ma^{tles}, my master's, letters, which he returned backe within two houres unbroken up, for want of titles also, especially that of *Potentissimo*, though there were enough for any Christian king. He sayd he would accept me as mediator, without other credence then a former letter, and desired me to write to his Matie for a new, for he could not be diminished in his honor. My Lord, I have only leysure to give you a generall tast of these fumes, and humbly to desire his Matie, both in these ceremonies and in the substance of busines, to suspend his creditt to any relation (for I have beene threatned with complaynts) untill I can have meanes to send an expresse, which I purpose to doe from Dansicke within ten dayes; for I have weighed all things, and, though I might have refused justly to enterpose my master's name where his letters were refused, yet necessitye both required my ayd; and I can give a good reason, that will satisfye his Matie, who is the patron only of the publicque good. For the ground of this war and the treatye of peace in the end thereof hath never beene rightly enformed, and I shall reveale many things to his Matie worthy the knowing, that are not beleeved, nor were once thought on (at least if I only were not deceived) in England. The treatye it selfe is drawne to narrow points: the substance is a truce for 6 yeares with an article obligatorie to treate a generall peace next yeare; that the King of

Swede shall surrender some Mediterran townes, and Marienburg, and the Heft [a] that doth command the Vistula; but it is over recompenced at the losse of the Marg. of Brandeburg *jure potentiæ*, by surrender of the Memel, a sea port, Fishehausen, and other places. The trade shalbe opened, though burthened with some charge, for the King of Swede will have a custome in the roade of Dansicke or els no truce. Here only lyes the difficultye, which will rest in me and our merchants to accommodate. Your Lordship may see the scope of the King of Swede to be master of all the ports and trade from the Narve to Stralsond, which is a matter of great consideration, and to hold all his profittable conquests, havens, and places neare the sea, at the charge of the trade and merchants and the losse of the Elector; for whosoever doth the wrong that prince must make the amends, who is unjustly undone, and it is thought meritorious (at least by the French Ambassador) to sacrifice a prince of our religion to the peace of the Romanist, for he is betweene the hammer and the anville, without help, being betrayed by his owne subjects for their barnes' sake. But I will by this conveyance forbeare to write much, and desire your Lordship to winne his Ma[ties] patience for me. I will give him an honest account of the care of his honor, of the interest of his estates, and of the publicque: so that I hope an impudent enemy shall not be able to except against me. But you wilbe pleased also with patience to heare what wee feele. There never was in the world such a distracted treaty, so many wrangles, so many parts, so many difficulties, so much wresting to partiall ends, but above all so much miserye in two camps. We treate from one army to another, now lodged in one, now in the other, in the field of Golgotha; the plague so hott in both that I never saw such a mortalitye in Turky, India, nor I thinke can be in Cayro, the seat of the plague, for the number. All the countrye is dispeopled; in 80 English mile not a house to sleepe safe in; no inhabitants except a few poore weomen and children *vertendo stercorarium* to find a corne of wheate. I

---

[a] The Frische Haff.

have begun to have my part, one of my kitchin being stroken dead; the French Ambassador hath lost 3; the King of Swede 60 servants of his bodye and all his cookes, many of his officers. Our new regiment of English halfe dead and not able to muster 200. Of all his Maties subjects, consisting of at least 13 regiments new and old, they cannot march 1500; more dye, or as many, of famine as of plague, inseparable companions; bread and water is the best dyet; and I heare nothing but lamentations, nor see varietye but of dead bodyes. My trayne and servants I sent at first to Dansicke, to save some, and I remayne with 4 only to doe my dutye, in more danger then the cannon doth threaten to ride betweene the camps to see an end of our labours, if God please to spare me. Howsoever, I will pursue my vocation, and trust in his providence. The King of Swede hath dispersed his army and is himselfe gone to the Pelow [a] to speake with the Elector and to take ship for Stockholme, of whome I have taken leave, and stand now in his favour, and he hath left us to fight it out against infection, weather, and famine. The Poles are retyred in not much lesse miserye foure Duch miles, easely parted if as easely agreed. I conclude nothing can goe right here, where ambition and glorie prevayle agaynst justice and modestye. I write in trouble, and therefore I desire your Lordship to excuse me both in the methode and matter and to keepe me in his Maties opinion as his most faythfull subject and your

Lordship's humble servant,

THO: ROE.

From miserable Elbing, worse than the Campe,
$\tfrac{7}{17}$ Sept. 1629.

[*Indorsed*] Copye of a letter to my Lord of Dorchester, dispatched by sea, 8 Sept. 1629, rec^d by Sir Rob. Anstruder's convayance the last of October, 1629.

[a] Pillau.

In a letter to Dorchester of $\frac{\text{Sept. 27,}}{\text{Oct. 7,}}$ Roe says that on Sept. $\frac{1}{1}$ he went to the Swedish camp near Marienburg to bring the Commissioners from both sides together on the next day. In the night came a protest from the French Ambassador disavowing in the name of the Poles "the principal ground of the treaty;" on which the Swedes angrily resolved to break off the negociation. Roe begged for delay, and in the morning went to the Polish camp and proposed another way of composition, and so brought the Commissioners to meet on the morning of Sept. $\frac{1}{1}$ in the fields of Altmark, half-way between the camps. At last they agreed on all points except "one of liberty of the Catholic religion in a town kept by the King of Sweden, in which both sides were so violent that we broke up in confusion, and returned in despair." In the night Roe argued with Oxenstjerna, and they both joined in writing to the King at Pillau. He then sent Gordon at midnight to the Poles to beg for a meeting on the $\frac{1}{1}$. After two days' discussion all was agreed on, when a new controversy arose between Roe and the French Ambassador about their masters' precedency in the form of treaty. At last it was agreed that they should both leave the camp at the same moment, and the Swedish and Polish Commissioners should do as they pleased without them. There was to be a truce till July 1, 1635, " with obligation of a new convention for a final peace the next year in some fit place to be agreed on with the Elector of Brandenburg." During this time the Vistula was to be freed, and the trade of Danzig, Königsberg, and Lithuania opened. The King of Poland's consent was still required to a new custom to be raised by the King of Sweden at Pillau and before Danzig. " I am glad," adds the writer, " to-morrow to go to Danzig, for this town," Elbing, " is a furnace of contagion, and I have walked these last days between death rather than between armies, lying in the field in such want, danger, and nastiness that it will offend any cleanly ear to hear." The King of Sweden met the Elector of Brandenburg at Fischhausen, and sailed on the $\frac{1}{4}$ for Calmar.

XIV. Sir Thomas Roe to Elizabeth, titular Queen of Bohemia.

MAY IT PLEASE YOUR MA^{tie},

It is as impossible for mee in a letter to give your Matie a relation of a moneths busines, as to expresse in words how full my humble heart is of thankfulnes to the King of Bohemia for the infinite favours and his affection shewed mee; and, if I should hope by prayses to your Matie to discharge some of a great debt, nothing is enough to say of so brave, just, religious, and benigne a prince, and

State Papers,
Poland.
Sept. 25
Oct. 5
1629.

therefore I will lett both alone and thanke God that he hath gotten
no harme where he could get no good. The substance of our
miserable treaty Mr. Carleton will relate to your Matie, and I have
only now intruded myselfe to kisse your Maties hands, and to lett
you know in generall that there is in the King of Swede a good
disposition, if wee knew how to employ it. He is a brave prince,
but wise to save himselfe, and maketh good private use of an opinion
and reputation that he is fitt to restore the publique. I dare say no
more by letter, but that wee see not well and distinctly in a per-
spective glasse at so great a distance. He hath given mee propositions and excellent grounds if the building thereon be not too
chargeable. In the meane time he seates himselfe fast in Prussia,
to the losse of the oppressed Prince of Brandeburgh, who hath a
strange fortune to be undone only by his friends, whereby in matter
of state wee have learned that too cold and stupid a neutrality is as
dangerous as lukewarmenes in religion; and he is become a grayne
of corne betweene two milstones, brused to make bread for others.
A French ambassador hath beene with him and made an ouverture
that I dare not write. I am made beleeve it is hotly negotiated,
but it is too good; all I can say is, that it is the best proposition for
your Matie that was ever projected, though the authors only looke
at themselves. I send it to his Matie in cyphar, for so I am entrusted.
That, and the King of Swede concurring, will reveiw all accounts
in Germany; but, when wee spend our selves heere to rayse brave
actions, they say you will prevent us with a peace that will rust all
our swords, so kind hearted is the Spanyard become, from whose
trust Almighty God deliver your Matie. By this time I doubt not
there is possession taken of that imployment wherein I ambitiously
desired to serve your Ma^ty, so that I cannot but justly complayne of
my starres that are alway canicular, especially in this, in which I
am sensible of wrong, having a promise, when I was sent to this
vally of death, that I should rest at the Haghe. If your Matie
doe not at least pitty mee, my wrong is doubled, though perhaps

you are better served. It is in vayne to lament, and nothing can now come worse to mee if your Matie once thinke that any man living doth more honor you or would more willingly dye to serve your Matie profitably or contentedly then,

Your Maties, I am sure, most antient and most humble servant.

Dansicke, 25 Sept. 1629.

XV. Sir Thomas Roe to Viscount Dorchester.[a]

MY VERY GOOD LORD,

I have more neede of an excuse for the historys I have sent your Lordship then to trouble you with additions. The best I have is this, that, falling upon disputes at my first arrivall, for which I was threatened with complaynts, and at my first entrye into busines a fame being spread that I perplexed the treatye, which they thought was almost ended, though I found the contrarye, I thincke it a duty to myselfe to sett downe faythfully the whole process, that not only his Matie may know what is done, but the reasons of my proceeding; for, as ther had beene no truce concluded if I had not made the temper and wonne both parts to consent to a moderate custome with the balance of our interest, so eyther the trade had beene overburthened or quite shutt up, whereas now the issue is that formerly the King of Swede, forcing all ships to come and sacrifice at the Pelow, and taking 10 and 12 in the 100 in the first rate, and 4 more in the valewation of the goods & money,[b] and as much outward, and if any of the same goods were transported to Dansicke as much more, and of those that came or laded immediatly at Dansicke 20 & 30 per 100. I hope to resettle the commerce

State Papers, Poland. Sept. 29 Oct. 9 1629.

---

[a] The letter is in two forms, one cyphered to a great extent, to be sent to England, the other a copy apparently kept by Roe. Where there is discrepancy the latter is followed, as a mistake may easily have occurred in the cyphering. The other form will be added in a note.

[b] "goods and" omitted in the other copy.

free at 5 in both ports, in specie, without loss upon mony or other imposition within land. Thus far we are in the generall treatye; ther rests only to dispose this citty to agreement, which I have done in the matter, though they will not declare nor article untill the King of Poland's licence doe warrant them, which done they cannot stand out alone, for, the treatye being ratefyed, they are concluded in the generall and must treate apart. In this I hope I have done his Matie and the publicque good service, and, if I did a little stand out that our merchants might be encouraged to returne hither, the King of Swede will find in experience that I have done him none ill, which he now beleeveth, and hath left the conclusion to me wholye, and he is at full libertye to use his virtue in any other place where he pleaseth. Your Lordship may cast away what superfluitye of my discourse you find impertinent, but I am persuaded there are woven in it many things the discoverye whereof are usefull, and his Matie may make his owne judgement out of your Lordship's notes and cast the rest into the fire. There rests onely that I enforme your Lordship of the motion of the French Ambassador to the Marquis of Brandeburg, mentioned in my relation. After some generall discourse of the feare of the house of Austria and their subduing of all Germany, he told the prince ther was but one remedy, to change the race and to elect a King of the Romans of another stocke, and asked herein his opinion, who answered, the motion was good and possible. Then he demanded if he would give his voyce if he saw the faction sure and strong, to which he replyed that when he was satisfyed in that he would answer. Then Charnassy told him that his Matie had employed him to that purpose in Germany, and offered the Duke of Bavare his help, who, after much argument, had accepted it; that three voyces were gayned, his owne, the Elector of Colen, and Triers, and that his would cast it, desiring his free declaration; to which the prince answered, that he could not with his oath of an Elector deliver before hand to whom he would give his suffrage untill they were mett in the Electorall Dyet, there to doe as God

and right did enspire him; but thus far he would engage himselfe,
that when he saw the Duke of Bavaria declare and were assured of
the two Bishops he would doe that [which] became a prince that
desired the liberty of Germany. Charnassy told him that the Duke
had promised his master three things if he were chosen: To admitt
the Protestant[a] religion within the empire with the same priviledges
so granted the Lutherans, who have liberty by the lawes, but the
other none; secondly, that he would restore the Dukes of Mekel-
burg, Pomern, Baden, and the free cittyes[b] to their inheritance;
thirdly, that he would recall the demand of ecclesiasticall livings
and grant them to the possessors without trouble; lastly, that he
would expell the stranger. To this offer that the ambassador asked
why he left out restitution of the Palatinate and the honours
annexed. To which he sayd he would promise nothing, but left
it to his consideration, that being elect King of the Romans or
Emperor he could not be Elector, and that in that case he would
treate with his cosen upon just and honourable tearmes. This was
the negociation of the French ambassador with his Highnes, who
doth beleeve the French King will pursue the dessigne, if ther be
no peace in Italie, Charnassy having order from hence to goe to the
Duke of Saxe. I pray God this be not a French nitingale that
sings sweetly but is all voyce. I cannot, I feare, returne this winter,
being enforced to stay in this towne to see the exsecution of the
treaty, which is here referred to me; which being done I must
necessarilye goe to Warsow to visitt the King, deliver my credence,
and negotiate the busines of the Duke of Curland, many complaynts
of our merchants, and to take off the Act of sealing our cloth at
this Dyett, which is a clogge upon the free commerce now established. Therfore I hope his Ma[tie] will command my Lord Treasurer
to send me mony, in which I beseech your Lordship to take care
of me and of the King's honor, for already I am deepe in myne owne

---

[a] *i.e.* the Reformed or Calvinist religion.
[b] "Duke of Pomerland, the Marquis of Baden, and the free citties," in the other copy.

creditt, and it is burthen enough to spend twice my allowance and not to add the lacke of that which my master gives me. In this and in all matters that concerne me I am confident of your Lordship's protection as the patron of

Your Lordship's most humble client and servant,

THO. ROE.

Dansicke, 29 Sept. 1629, old stile.

Mr. Gordon, who hath taken great paynes, humbly desires your Lordship's assistance with my Lord Treasurer, that he may not in this cold countrye live like a cameleon. I desire your Lordship that my journall may not be seene but to those that love truth or me.

I beseech your Lordship to send me his Maties resolution what he pleaseth to command me, and to procure my licence to come home, and to direct me what way I shall take, if he have any service for me. I hope his Matie will make some other choyce for the generall treatye next yeare, for if I be stayed I shalbe undone at this allowance. His Matie will heare from the Kings and the Elector of the tyme and place, and wilbe invited to continue his mediation; but a person of greater qualetye and a better purse will befitt so great an office, and I hope his Matie will looke upon me according to that promise, that he would employ me nearer, and not keepe me ever a stranger to my deare countrye.

XVI. Sir Thomas Roe to the King.

State Papers,
Poland.
Sept. 30
Oct. 10
1629.

MAY IT PLEASE YOUR MA^{tie}

How far I have proceeded in obedience to your Maties commands I have largely enformed my Lord of Dorchester; how well, wholy despends upon your meere grace and acceptance. I may doubt some preventing rumors may have out runne my diligence, for feare did not lend me wings, there being nothing so bold as a good con-

science before a just master. But I have written truth, and, like a faythfull wittnes, the whole truth, as well circumstances as matters; that your Matie may take and reject, approve and condemne what you please. It is enough for me, if any thing I have done be gratious, and that for the rest I may have pardon. Your Matie will find some thing new, for we see not so perfectly by the best perspectives as at nearer distances with the naturall eye. If therefore I have in an unexpected cause any way exceded, the humble zeale of your Maties honour hath beene the worst of my errors; yet I may say I have seene a brave king and a glorious capteyne that hath high Pyrrean thoughts which he wilbe ready to act in your Maties and the publicque service. I have so neare done when I returne from Varsow, that I will presume to crave leave, and begg your Maties revocation and to receive your Royall pleasure, haveing a burthen too heavye for weake shoulders to beare long, under which I will yet willingly sincke while it carrieth the title of your Maties service, wherein no man shall more gladly dye then
 Your Maties most loyall subject and humble servant,
            Tho. Roe.
Dansicke, 30 Sept., 1629, old stile.

XVII. Sir Thomas Roe to Viscount Dorchester.

My very good Lord,

By a gentleman sent expresse I gave your Lordship account of my actions and the generall affayres to the 20 Sept. my arrivall to this citty being desired by the Commissioners of both parts to accommodate what remayned to the perfection of the treaty betweene the King of Swede and the Dansickers. With him I addressed to your Lordship divers letters to his Ma^ty, the coppy of the articles, an enformation of the Elector of Brandeburg, and one to your Lordship of the 30 Sept. which being I hope safely arrived I shall not neede to looke backe. The state of the truce I left depending upon the ratification of the King of Pole and a declaration that he did consent that this towne should treate for the

[marginal note: State Papers, Poland. Oct. 14, 1629.]

customes demanded by the Swede apart. Since which both are come to Elbing, engrossed and signed the one, the other by word of mouth, which was as much as was required. So that on that side all is well and really performed. But in my absence Coll. Doenhoff, that brought the ratification, would not deliver it without receiving the other deposited in my hands, for which both he and the Chancelor wrote to me, and yesterday I sent Mr. Gordon to performe that trust. So that I esteeme the truce betweene the crownes perfected, and that the reddition of townes and forts shall presently be putt in execution. But the French amb^r, in whose hands the one part is, hath made a new difficulty to consigne it, because in the forme of of that of the Swede his Ma^{ty} is styled King of France, which being done by the Commissioners in the feilds when we left them, referring our selves to their discretion, and he after discovering, practised to gett it into his power, and to that purpose procured a warrant from the Poles Commissioners to compare them, pretending essentiall differences in the writing, which when he could not have, being in my keeping, he desired a coppy, and there in the margent of that title wrote *nec est, nec esse debet*, and protested he would never surrender nor assist in the transaction if those words were not rased or a new written. Upon which occasion the Chancelor of Swede sent a secretarye to mediate with me, but I made a short answere to all their fallacious propounded temperaments, that being once and rightly so done and both bound to stand to what should be done, with liberty onely of protestation, I would change nothing, especially to doe an act and to consent to that which the French witt would draw into consequence, as a renunciation, assuring the Chancelor the French King would never treate with the King of Spaine on condition to leave out the title of Navarre; therefore that I would deliver myne as I received it without alteration, except he would consent to alter all and putt in my name before Mr. Charnace. And this order I gave in writing to Mr. Gordon, to make the assignation without any change; which what wrangle and delay it will breede I cannot foresee, but I hope the interested will fulfill the truce and leave us to our owne quarrells. There is risen likewise another difference, for the King of Pole, ratefying the generall treatye, was assured by his Commissioners that the Elector of Brandeburg should of his owne charge pay the garrisons of Marienburg and the Heft, and render to him the profitts of the territorye, a condition most unjust, which promise they exact of Mr. Charnace in these words by their letter, *agitur de fide vestra*, and he doth now deny that he did undertake it, but onely that he would doe his endeavour; by which it may be discerned whither his desires enclined, to make the Marquiss the ransome of the peace. And thus he doth trouble our conclusion more then ever he advanced it, and did seeme to advance *in fretta* at my comming, by promising without authority or commission, being often since disavowed. But I hope this will not hinder the publicque, being a contention betweene the King and the Duke of Prussia, which the French must reconcile as he is able. But it is cleare to me that the whole negotiation had this scope; to reconcile the crownes to recover the Romish and ecclesiasticall lands, and, having little or no trade in these parts, to buy and redeeme these at the charge of the trade, eyther to leave it as it was, for the King of Swede to take what he pleased, or that such rates should be imposed in Dansicke as might discourage the merchant and overburthen the commerce, and consequently the materialls of our shipping and navigation consume, while the cardinall did meditate a greatnes in the sea, which I hope shall never be build upon our decay. In the matter of the trade I have written to Alderman Clotherow what I doe as concerning the merchant, who will satisfie your Lordship, if you please to call him, or send for my letter. There rests onely that is materiall to the full consummation of the truce and opening of the commerce, to dispose these senators to agree with the Swede, wherein I have little advanced. The last weeke I mett the Chancelor at the Heft to draw him to moderate demands and to forme articles, wherein as he is unprofitably covetous so I can gett no resolution here, though they dayly consult. The *Centumviri* have declared with me, but some of the great councell, partiall to themselves and angry for the loss of their farmes on the Neringe,[a] trouble all. But in conclusion they must yeild, and their delay hath hurt the publicque, for now they must treate *precario*, the generall treaty being ratifyed, and they having excluded themselves by neglect or malice, unlesse they will make war alone and shutt up their owne port, which they cannot nor dare doe for feare of their people, which crye for peace. But I now finde what vexation and tediousnes it is to deale with a mixed government, where suspition and jealousye is wisedome, and with whom every thing hath lost his favour that is propounded from a supposed enemye. They would not beleeve that the ratification should be, and therfore they lost their oportunity and must now redeeme it, which they better endure then reason, *estant enclins à esperer plus qu'ils ne doivent et à endurer moins qu'il n'est necessaire.*

I would willingly say somewhat of the King of Swede and what he is like to undertake, having *les coudees franches,* but I may doe wrong, whither my letters pass safe or not; only so much I will adventure, that he doth not disarme nor licence one troope, but rather endeavours to fill up the weake, and to take as many new upon him as will present themselves. The report of the truce being come to Wallestein, he hath, as it [is] written, recalled some regiments dessigned for Italie, fearing he shalbe forced *rationem reddere* in the spring, in which I say no more then that I beleeve. His Ma[tie] may make it sure if it concurre with his dessignes, and that it were a great dullness to know good councells when their oportunys is escaped. Your Lordship I hope will pardon me this flash of zeale to the publicque.

I sett forward to Varsow at the Dyett beginning the 3 Nov., a miserable flight in winter, all wayes being infected. At my returne, proposed in 16 dayes, I will endeavour to recover Hamburgh, and so home, if I receive no other order, which I pray your Lordship prevent, for my mony is spent, and my creditt fayled, if my Lord Treasurer doe not satisfye Borlemachy, and therfore I hope your

[a] The spit of land in front of the Frische Haf.

SIR THOMAS ROE'S MISSION. 49

Lordship will move his Ma{tie} to repayre me or I shall suffer more then modesty will confess; and so I leave your Lordship to the gratious keeping of our blessed God, resting

Your Lordship's devoted humble servant,
THO. ROE.

Dansicke 1̶3̶ Oct. 1629.

If her Ma{tie} the Queene please to have toyes of amber, as cabinetts, glasses, bason and cawre, cups, boules, tankers, boxes to furnish a cupboard, if I may know her pleasure and may have mony, I shalbe most diligent to doe her humble service.

[*Indorsed by Dorchester*] Recd the 23 of 9{ber} st{o} n{o} 1629.

XVIII. *Sir Thomas Roe to Sir Robert Carr.*

SIR,

When such a brother returnes to you who hath been present at all our wrangling busines and is as well able to relate and judge as any man, I should not neede to write for any cause but my owne; yet, seing no letter can be so welcome to you as that which comes by his hand, I would not omitt to doe this the grace, which els hath no other meritt. I know not how the game of State is playd, nor the *arcana* of our present negotiations in England, and therefore what soever I may propose is as like to miss as hitt; at the best perhaps I can doe little good, and in the other hurt myselfe; yet, knowing both your wisedome and sinceritye to his Ma{ties} service, which I esteeme the publicque and know no distinction, and your nearnes to his person, to be able to make fitt use of every intimation and to give it tyme and season, it were a sullen reservednes and a betraying of truth to forbeare to tell you that this brave king, having made a truce and yet seeks to encrease his army, must have some nobler dessigne then to wast idle, or in this corner of the world. He is a prince highly ambitious of glory and dominion

State Papers,
Poland.
Oct. 28
Nov. 7.

and hath no object before him but the war of Germany, whither a
little reall encouragement from England would transport him; if
therefore his Matie hath use of such a capteyne who is prosperous,
triumphing, and the best discipliner in Europe, one that hath the
singular grace to content his followers without mony, because he is
commiles with every man, and gives besydes excellent words and
good usage as much as he hath, now is the oportunitye to sett him
up, which being omitted seldome returnes, as tyme. I dare not
dilate upon the severall conjunctures of the declaration of France,
the success of the Hollanders, the union of the Protestant cantons,
the oppression of the Grisons, the discontent of the two lay Electors
and ambition of the third, all at once conspiring agaynst the common enemye, who hath nothing left, no sanctuarye, but the worne
out craft of retyring to a treatye; wherein, if they become my
master's true friends upon good ground, I am their servant; and I
say no more, but *esse dolum in fide hostis*, and I desire you to
smother my meditations and to take me into your protection so far
as to beleeve, and to assist to maynteyne the same beleefe in his
Matie, that if my witt were equall to my zeale I should never offend
him. You cannot lose by doeing a good office, because it requites
itselfe, and I can promise for myselfe no more then that I am

         Your faythfully devoted servant.

Dansicke, 28 Oct. s.v. 1629.

XIX. *Sir Thomas Roe to Viscount Dorchester.*

R. H. MY VERY GOOD LORD,

State Papers, Poland. Oct. 29 Nov. 8 1629.

The French ambassador refusing to deliver the articles signed
and the plenepotence deposited in his hands to the Suede for the
capricio mentioned, in a storme of passion sent them backe and
rendered them to the Poles, which hindered the execution of the
treaty 8 dayes: in so much that we were forced to send to the
campe to receive the one part and consigne the other; which being
done with all good fayth, both sides tooke great offence at this his

proceeding, not to performe the publicque trust, and he is gone away discontent, without further ceremonye. Since the truce is proclaymed in all parts but this cittye, wherein there is a faction of discord, men who seeke what they dare not find, a scandall to renew the troubles. The articles betweene the Senate and the Swede I have drawne, and so filed them that ther rests only a convention to polish them: something remayning on both parts, which they reserve, as I hope, to abate one the other, as an earnest of the new friendship; but I feare the conclusion must be deferred untill my returne from the Parliament at Varsaw, being the $\frac{3}{13}$ November, for without a stickler they will neyther agree nor meete. In the meane tyme the subtill Chancellor of Swede doth *frui diis iratis*, and takes occasion at their stomach to fill his owne: and to exact the unjust and heavy customes of the war to their owne, ours, and the publicque loss and prejudice, in which I have contested with him; but, pretending that the truce is not consummate and the tyme of shipping now almost out of season, he will not change as he pretends the bookes, and in friendship doth us this wrong; the Poles enjoying the fruictes of peace and we and the Hollanders involved in the obstinacye of Dansicke, in which I doubt ther hath beene some leaven of the Jesuits; wherin the wicked shall not prosper; for I will not leave untill I have settled all according to my former intimation to your Lordship, in which, if the merchant find his custome too heavye, his Matie and the States may resent it as a case apart, when the truce hath taken vigour, as a surcharge on their subjects, who have not merited to beare the punishment and to pay the price of others quarrells. This wilbe easy to amend if the King of Swede continue in peace; and if he transport his army into Germanye, to which end I hope he hath layd this foundation to defray the warr at the lost[a] of the trade, it is not ill bestowed on him. On the 26 of this moneth began the reddition of the townes and forts, and by the end, I suppose, all wilbe transacted betweene the crownes.

[a] *Sic.*

The King of Swede doth give new commissions and seekes all wayes to fill and encrease his forces: certeynely not *pour faire la monstre* nor to conquer toward the North Pole; but he is exasperated by Wallestein, who hath lately both assayled his ships in the sea and by land, made an attempt on Stralsont, where he lost 800 men, and ther is no prince in Europe more unlike to swallow an affront patiently. Therfore, if ever ther be dessigne to use this prosperous capteyne, now is the tyme, when his owne bloud and occasions provoke him and the conjuncture of all Christendome doth invite him, and ther is nothing wanting but a little reall encouragement; for I am perswaded, though he may doe some act of bravado in Pomerland the next yeare, yet without good seconds he will not far be engaged, and that his only ayme is the rest of the sea ports; and if he be not employed the next quarrell wilbe betweene him and Denmarke.

By Mr. Rankin I neyther received his Ma[ties] nor your Lordship's commands, nor creditt nor comfort, and my ignorance of the secretts of the treatyes, diversly noysed here, doe keepe me in awe, having no will to cross any contemplation of my master; yet I cannot forbeare to say that too much good nature is as much to be suspected in an old enemye and a wise, who doth alway march *unâ viâ* though not *uno gradu*, as open hatred, *esse dolum in fide hostis*. But for me to miss that have no grounds to know is no wonder, and therfore I will only pray that, seeing now both wayes are in equall degree offered his Majestie, that he may chose like Soloman that which may include other unseene blessings.

The Prince Elector of Brandeburgh hath earnestly desired me to resollicite his Ma[tie] to recommend his affayres to the Lords the States according to the enformation sent your Lordship, that he fall not into the danger of the Emperor, which, being an office agreeable to his royall inclination to releeve the oppressed, I know you wilbe pleased to remember and to give order therein.

I understand that a good friend of myne, Mr. Robert Brantwayt, hath his hopes depending on your Lordship to procure him a re-

compence of his long service. I am not easely drawne to write for others, and to spend that favour I may neede for my selfe, but I owe his honestye so much that I must share with him, and will presume to entreat your Lordship to thinke that what you doe for him I take it done to my selfe, and that you shall oblige two at once, one that will pray for you and another that will not dye ungratefull though he prove your
     Lordship's unprofitable and humble servant,
            THOMAS ROE.
Dansicke, 29 Oct. S. V. 1629.

[*Indorsed*] R. Whitehall, 22 of December.

On Nov. $\frac{1}{5}$ Roe set out from Danzig and reached Warsaw on Nov. $\frac{14}{24}$. On Dec. $\frac{7}{17}$ he was back at Danzig.

XX. Elizabeth, titular Queen of Bohemia, to Sir Thomas Roe.

HONEST THOM,

  This worthie gentleman did deliver me your letter when I was at the Busse,[a] and when I came hither I did receave another from you, which did lett me know all your proceedings. I had given you then thankes for them and that you sent me from Amsterdam, but a feaver which took me sudainlie did hinder my writing; it made me very weake for the time, and I was cured by being lett blood. As soone as I was well I went to Rene to aire myself, and now I ame come home I tell you all this, that you may not think that I have forgotton you by my long silence, for assure yourself I will ever be constantlie honest fatt Thom's true frend in spite of the divell. I ame sorie you have had so uncomfortable a journey; I hope one day all shall be recompenced to your advantage, at least I shall both wish it and doe my best to have it so. Sr Henry Vane is at the last arrived heere and this day hath had his audiance. He hath brought

State Papers, Poland. Nov. $\frac{5}{15}$, 1629.

---

[a] Hertogenbosch or Bois-le-Duc.

from my brother the oulde kinde message to us that he will never make peace with Spaine without our full restitution. Cottington [a] was at the sea side to be gone, and the Lyon, that brought Vane over, is gone to fetch Don Carlo Columna [b] into England. Harry Vane was hastened away uppon the speecke of theyr making heere a truce, either to hinder it or else to make it jointlie together. He tells us that my brother is fullie resolved to have a quick answere one way or other and will not be drawen one [c] to loose more time. I leave you to thinke of all this as you will. And now for more waightie affaires. Our hunting at Rene was verie good, where Rura lost much leather and her hatt, and satt bare a whole day, to the great hinderance of her ease. We have now heere verie good companie and are in great hope to have the French players heere, and verie good fooling this winter. I wish you out of Barbarie, that you were heere in ordinarie.[d] I will not forgett to doe you all the good offices I can to our fatt ambassador, that you may be his successour, and be assured you have not a frend that wisheth you better then doth Your most constant frend,

ELIZABETH.

The King desires you to be assured of the same from as I say for myselfe I can witnes with him that he loves you verie well. Robin Honiwood hath his troope of horse. Either burne this or keepe it safe.

The Hagh, $\frac{9}{19}$ of November.

[*Addressed*] To Sir Thomas Roe, Ambassadour for the King of Great Britaine in Dansique.

[a] Going as ambassador to negotiate peace.
[b] Don Carlos Coloma, so frequently miswritten Colonna by English writers.
[c] *i.e.* on.
[d] As ordinary ambassador here.

XXI. Sir Thomas Roe to Viscount Grandison.

MY LORD,

I am newly returned from Varsaw, where I have beene as bravely received and honored as any ambassador hath beene or can be in any court. There I have obteyned his Maties desires, or at least putt them into a right way, both for the Duke of Curland and other affayres of re-establishing the trade. I chose the tyme of their Parlament assembled to ratefye the truce to constitute new Commissioners for the generall treatye, and to pay the army, which are all decreed with much confusion, usuall in their dyetts, where they feast all the tyme, and doe all busines tumultiously the two last dayes. In this court I have observed two things remarkable, the wisedome and patience of an old King, *dominationis peritus*. Your Lordship knowes there is no people boast so much of their libertye, which is indeed alway great: but especially used in their Parlaments, where they doe talke and threaten, and vant and oppose, beyond all rule or example; yet the experienced King getts his ends of them and governs absolutly by suffering them to runne themselves weary and out of breath without contradiction, but rather subtilly flattering and bearing their licenciousnes and soothing them in the pleasure they take to speake; when they can say no more, by tyme and patience he doth in conclusion what he please. My second observation is not unlike it, his art to weaken our religion and yet never to persecute it; for that is against libertye, their mistris, more beloved then religion. When he came to the crowne, the greatest part of the Senate were Protestants, and much of the nobilitye; now in the one there are but two, among the other very few, whom he hath worne out by a constant rule; that, as he never troubled any for religion, so he never makes senator, nor gives the benefitts of the crowne, being wholy in his disposition, to any but Papists. Thus the Protestant hath no exception against him, for grace is free; and they seeme to enjoy libertye that brings them to beggerry; for the great wealth of the gentry depends upon

State Papers, Poland. Dec. 18/28 1629.

the crowne land, which the King must give, and upon great offices, neyther of which he ever bestowes on those of our profession. Other persecution would have made them encrease, bred zeale in them and pitty in others toward them, and perhaps for the common love of libertye help from the adversarye, who now pine away and by long continuance of tyme in one constant course are content to lett their children governe their conscience by their hope of wealth and preferment; and the Papist, having the benefitt, is content to lett the other enjoy the ready path of loosing. By this meanes a greater mutation is wrought in this state in matter of religion then in France by the sword, in Italye by the Inquisition, or in England by pecuniarye lawes, which are bought and sold like the Popes' bulls and pardons; and I am perswaded, if the like course were taken with our recusants 20 yeares, that they enjoyed nothing but the benefitt of subjects and the law, that they had neither favour nor place in court nor common-weale, their ambition and stomacke would wind them about sooner then persecution, for nothing doth more worke upon men then contempt and to be lett alone as unconcerned and unworthy of equaletye with others. Honour and the belly hath a great stroke in this world, and when man doth know before hand he cannot rise, before he declare and be hardened he will fitt his conscience to his life. To leave my meditations and come nearer home; I have finished all my busines, I am sure with great paynes and danger and to the honor of my master and the publicque benefitt. If it may find proportionable acceptance it wilbe a comfort, though no reward. Some differences yet depend betweene the King of Swede and this citty, which concerne the trade, which I hope to compose. But overtaken with winter, and no shipping left, I must rest here untill February or March, that the seas be open. His Ma[tie] hath commanded me to pass by Denmarke for his service, where I will doe my duty though the occasion is overslipt; and I feare only my owne zeale hath made the expectation too great; but I will trye my art, and to have made a fayre offer can be no offence.

The King of Swede giveth new commissions and reenforceth his army to 30,000 foote and 8,000 horse; mony he hath none to pay them, therfore your Lordship may expect to heare of him in a place where the soldier hath beene taught to live without pay. Sure I am that now were the oportunitye to make the common enemye stoope, and to grace our ambassadors, that treate peace. He is a most brave aspiring prince, *ad magnos res et mutationes natus*. I will not further trowble your Lordship till I may have the happines to discharge my heart to you, that is full of observations and above all things devoted to doe you service. Almighty God give your Lordship health.

Your Lordship's most humble servant,

TH. R:

Dansicke, 10 Dec. 1629.

On Dec. $\frac{14}{24}$ Roe wrote to the King that he was delayed. The Elector of Brandenburg had begged him to meet him, as Oxenstjerna "had made a transaction of all the territories of Danzig beyond the Vistula, contrary to the sense and expounded meaning of the treaty; wherupon the King of Poland hath appointed new Commissioners to complain and protest, and ther is great cause to fear a confusion of business." Again, on Jan. $\frac{9}{19}$, he wrote that Oxenstjerna still refused to meet the deputies of the city, "and unless the King of Sweden purpose to use that which he will exact of the public, as he hath long pretended, I see no cause so much to yield to him, which the State of Holland doth begin to feel sensibly, the King of Denmark utterly to dislike, and under which the free cities do groan. I have here heard a report that the States of Sweden assembled in Parliament have remonstrated that their kingdom is exhaust of men and money, and that is true; that they have shorn themselves to aid their King against his enemy, but that with the Emperor and Germany they have neither quarrel nor interest; and therefore they desire to be excused to be engaged in a new war. This perhaps may be what the Imperialls wish, and cannot aver it, but I know the new levies are superseded."

XXII. *Sir Thomas Roe to Viscount Dorchester.*

RIGHT HON^ble MY VERY GOOD LORD,

I have lately oppressed your Lordship with letters and narrations, if at least they pass safely, for I have not knowne that any one sent your Lordship is come to hand since my departure from Copen-

State Papers, Poland. Jan. 24 Feb. 3 1629-30.

hagen, though I have written many and by divers wayes; of whose safe arrivall I should be glad to heare, especially of a great packet by Mr. Gordon's servant of the 19 Sept. with a large relation of the circumstances and passages of the treatye of truce, with the articles and letters of divers princes to his Matie, which if it have miscarried will make all that followed descure, having reference to matters supposed to be foreknowne. A catalogue of all I insert in the margen, that your Lordship may find what is missing. In my last I gave account of such collections as I had made of the King of Swede's resolution to goe into Pomerland and the contrarye, for the probabilityes are great both wayes, and he will declare to none in any confidence but where he may draw profitt. In that letter I promised your Lordship to endeavour by conference with the Chancellor of Swede (being to remove to Elbing to order the treatye with Dansicke) to discover more, whereon to rayse a judgement, which is the subject of this letter. The proceedings and success of the convention of the Commissioners of Swede and Dansicke, this day begun, shalbe the matter of another, that breathing betweene they may both seeme the less tedious.

I must begin first with a narration of all the conferences I have had with the Chancelor since my arrivall here, and of other gatherings, observations, and advises that concerne this busines, or reflect upon yt, that from the whole I may draw a conclusion of my sense and opinion, humbly submitting it to his Matie and hoping it may be usefull by application to other treatyes, or by taking a fitt oportunitye (which wilbe offered) to use the virtue, conduct, and prosperitye of this brave king.

I desired the Chancelor to cleare me in the various reports of the preparations of his King for Germanye, being necessary for them, that their friends might conforme with them at least for good correspondence and the encrease of mutuall confidence betweene their Maties our masters; and, whither war or peace were resolved, to distinguish to me the latitude of their purposes, eyther to make the war for the generall cause or for the Kyngs owne interest of

Meckelburgh and the Balticque sea, without the securitye whereof I know he will never thinke himselfe safe in Swede, and ther is no prince that foreseeth more penetrating and preparing *a longè futuris rebus*, except only the Spaniard, who lookes as far as Domesday, wherin he scarce beleeveth; or, in case of making peace, what ease, comprehension, or advantage the publicque might expect from yt.

He protested that he could assure nothing but only that his King was fully purposed at his departure to carry his army into those parts for his owne interest, and there to proceede according to occasions eyther of the access and ayd of his friends or the strength and actions of his enemies. In which resolution he knew no change. I told him what rumors were spread of a beginning of a treatye with the Emp^r and such particulars as he must kuow came from himselfe, hoping he would more freely discover that which he saw he could not safely nor handsomely dissemble. Then he confessed that he had received letters from his King, that there were overtures made of peace from the Emperor, and that the King of Denmarke had offered himselfe as a mediator, but upon what conditions he pretended ignorance of any declaration authentically from his master; but by other wayes he sayd he had beene advertissd that the Ansiaticque townes had resolved to enterpose, and that to that end one Mons. Walleran, formerly employed by Wallstein in the treatye betweene the Emperor and Denmarke, had beene sent privatly to confer with some friends of the King of Swede to sound the foord, by which meanes and with what hope they might proceede. The first poynt propounded was: the Swede could not make peace with his owne securitye unless he were freed of all feares and care in the Balticque sea, to which this explorator answered that the Emperor would give him full satisfaction. The other replyed, that the King of Swede did expect realityes and fact and would trust upon no promises nor written securityes in a matter that concerned his safetye. Whereunto Walleran sayd, that also should be done and the Imperiall fleete dissolved. The friends answered that was not sufficient as long as the ports remayned in their power; ships did growe and might be repayred when opportunitye required. And it was replyed in that also they should have content, and that Wismar and Rostock should be sett at libertye and restored *pristino statu*. The other, following the streame, sayd that they did not thinke the King was secure with the surrender of those townes, nor could with his honor abandon the Princes of Meckelburgh, his nearest kinsmen, nor would make any peace without their full restitution. To which Walleran answered, that was a hard knott not so easely untyed, in respect of the investiture and the meritt of Wallestein both to the Emp^r and Empire, but if a treatye were constituted he did not doubt there might be found some temper and accomodation; upon which conference it was written that some Amb^r were dessigned to goe to his master, eyther from the King of Denmarke or the Hans-townes or both, but that he did not know of any arrived to that end. This the Chancelor professed was all he could say, and this later dialogue not from his master, and therfore he gave it no other creditt then an ordinarye rumour (and I thinke he told it me to gett an appetite in us), but if any such offer were made that he thought his king would resolve according to the propositions and the securitye of them, or his owne meanes and occasions.

I earnestly moved him to declare ingeniously his own opinion and what he thought of his master's inclination and ends and what were those occasions that might incline him to peace or war. He answered that all the world did know and must beleeve that his King had just cause and fervent desire to have his revenge of the Emperor both for his particular and the publicque. In his particular, for the safetye of his owne kingdome, and in requittall of the coloured invasions and ayds sent by the Emperor against him, and for respect of the house of Meckelburgh so neare allyed to him, whose destruction he could not well digest, and the oppression of his unckle the Bishop of Bremen. For the publicque, in the first place, for the releife of the Electoral Palatine, with which formerly the kings and crownes of Swede had kept strict correspondence

and were united by antient offices of love above all other in
Germanye. And particularly for the cause of the King of
Bohemia, for whom he was willing to expose his life and fortune.
But that it did not become the wisedome of his master to embrace
so great a quarrell alone, knowing his owne strength unable to
oppose the whole house of Austria and the Empire. For that
which concerned his owne interest, and that of the Princes of
Meckelburgh comprehended in yt, he did assure himselfe the King
would provide for his safetye eyther by war or treatye, as his owne
occasions and necessityes should direct him; because, being alone
and depending on his owne counsells, he knew whereto to trust, and
might take or leave, proceede or retyre, without the offence of any
and *sine periculo tentare fortunam*, having his owne ships and a
port open. But to enter into the generall quarrell (though his
desires and courage did invite him, and that he was willing to
spend all his meanes, eaven to some hazard of his owne), without
being assured by confederacye of a sufficient ground to goe thorough
the war and to be able to beare some check or adversitye, he
thought no friend would counsell or expect it from him. But if he
might be supplyed with means in a generall war directed to one
scope and end and constantly prosecuted by a league, in which case
he could not retyre nor take conditions for himself without generall
consent, that, as he did beleeve the King would embrace it above all
other dessignes, so he, the Chancellor, would counsell him not to
make any peace in Pomerland, but to give the glorye to his crowne
to have beene *Restitutor Germaniæ*. I desired him to intimate to
me what confederation it was, and what proportion he did expect
that might content his King,. for that the generall propositions given
me to send to his Matie were so vast and unlimited that no certeynty
could be extracted out of them. Because the world did report and
beleeve that already the King had entered into league and conditions with the French and the States of the United Provinces,
which if it were true it were requisite to acquaynt my master freely,
that he might concurre and conforme his counsells and actions to

the common end. He answered that ther was no such thing done, that it was true the French ambassador had proposed to contribute monye and pretended to have full power to treate, but when it was examined he wanted power to conclude. That when he went from hence in Oct. last he reported he had received new commission of plenepotence; but being arrived in Swede it was found so generall, consisting of offers and declarations of his king's desire and projects of diversions, that nothing could be made of it. And that therfore he was dispatched with this answere & no more, that if the French King did really purpose any such matter that he should give absolute power to his ambassador resident at the Haghe, & that the King of Swede would doe the like to Camerarius to treate, conclude, and bind.

For Holland it was likewise true that his master had given commission to his resident and Falkenberg to negotiate a confederacye, and to that purpose he had entered into particular offers, but during the summer the States were so embroyled in the war and since so perplexed with diversitye of opinions for peace, that the motion had layne asleepe and nothing fully determined. That it was further true the King had beene invited by the Duke of Wirtenburg, some other princes, and free townes, but no resolution nor proportion declared, but generalityes and concurrence, to which his master could not trust. That in the Elector of Saxe there was no hope, in Brandenburgh uncerteynty what he would resolve or was able to performe. In generall, that now all did depend upon the new treaties of the Haghe, for if they made peace it would wholly alter not only the state of affayres, but the thoughts of all the princes in Germanye. But that, if the kings and princes did desire that his master should undertake the cause, first he would esteeme it a great contribution to be assured that the French would constantly prosecute the war in Italie & not make peace alone, though he gave the less. Secondly, that the States should be obliged to continew the war & to exercise the Spaniard untill the treatyes might be generall, and that then if his Matie for his part would make a league (into which he was assured many princes & citties would enter & contribute accordingly to their abilitye) he did then know his master would joyne with them, or els that he must accomodate to his owne meanes & occasions. But above all things, if he should embrace the war, with this condition, that he might be secured of the King of Denmarke, whom he knew the Emperor would stir up to divert him & of whom he had most jealousye, wherein he thought the authoritye of his Matie both for propinquitye of bloud and other meanes to restreyne the King from any such attempt would be of most efficacye.

Since this conference Zavadsky the Poles' secretarye told me that he heard at the court the Emperor would take the advantage of the article in the generall truce to be comprehended on that syde, and had signifyed privatly that within the tearme of 5 monethes limited therein he would publicquely declare, which is another ground of a treatye.

In another occasion of answering an objection of the Poles, that the Swedes' horse were not drawn out of Prussia, according to the treatye, the Chancelor told me, *in confidentiâ*, that he had made such excuses as he could, but to them he might not give the true reason, which was that they were kept togither to march into Pomerland in the spring, on which his master was resolved for divers necessityes.

At a second meeting he acquaynted me with an advice that the King of Denmarke did arme & rayse troopes, which did much perplexe him, & desired me to communicate what I had heard & what I did judge therof. To which I answered that I had received the like news, but that I could not imagine it was done in any prejudice or opposition of his master, which would be odious to all Germanye. Besides, that the King of Denmarke was a prince that highly prized his honour, he could not be so blinded in judgement as to ayd or trust the house of Austria. I gave him assurance of that King's profession to me in my last negotiation with him, that he had not made peace in despayre of the common cause, nor with so full satisfaction that he might not in good occasion review the accounts. That therfore ther was no subject of umbragiousnes, first because the troopes were few, such as were only fitt for defence & garison. Secondly, that the King of Denmarke, beleeving his master would descend in Pomerland, and knowing that the war would draw neare his frontyre, every wise prince would stand upon his guard & prevent a surprise: that especially the King of Denmark had reason so to doe, because after the departure of the Imperiall troopes the last spring he had seased Femeren and many places of the bishopricque within Holstein, which he must eyther quitt to the enemye or prepare to defend. Lastly, that, the pretensions of his sonnes being not renownced, he might hope to find by the help of the King of Swede an oportunitye to advance them, but that ther was any thought to check or divert the glorious enterprises of his master, which were directed principally in favour of the Princes of Meckelburgh & for the libertye of the Balticque sea, in both which the interest, profitt, & safetye of both kings was common, no man of common sense could beleeve or conceive. He replyed that he hoped so, and that the letters of the King of Denmarke to his master upon his last peace were loving and full of assurance of good vicinitye. But yet an antient accumulation and some late passages were not free of suspicion. First, he sayd, ther was lately an ambassador arrived with his King from Denmark, with a sleeveless message concerning the indiscreet busines of the Rhyngrave (wherof your Lordship may have heard, for I will not soyle my paper with it), which he did not thinke worthy of so much care, nor that the King of Denmarke would in earnest draw it into any dispute or consequence, but that the colour was taken to observe the preparations and to discover his masters counsells. Secondly, that the King of Denmarke had since written to persuade & mediate a peace, which showed no affection to see their troopes in Germanye. Lastly, that the Secretarye Gonthier had made divers journyes & had sundrye secrett conferences vith Walstein, which were purposely disguised & hid from Sir Rob[t] Amstruther & were yet unpenetrated.

To all these jealousies I gave such answeres as my present cogitations could present. In conclusion he seemed satisfyed, yet with this restriction, that his master would not embrace the generall quarrell without securitye of that king by the mediation of his Matie, which, though it may be suspected for a subterfuge, yet the prevention in the first place is worthy of his Maties care and consideration; and that in case of prosecuting his owne privat interest in Meckelburgh he would also leave sufficient garrison to defend his owne, for nothing was more dangerous to any prince then to trust to others when he may trust himselfe.

This is all I can present to your Lordship on which to ground your owne judgement & of which in this conjuncture of treatyes I suppose you may draw some profitt, and because the busines doth appeare intricate, the discourses counteying probabilityes both wayes, according to my promise, I will give my opinion, humbly submitting it to your Lordship's correction. In all my observations and practice in these parts, from many circumstances, I have resolved that the King of Swede did intend conquest and enlargement of his dominion, but especially to be master of this sea, the ports & trades therein, & from thence to rayse himselfe a revenew, to maynteyne the one without charge of the crowne of Swede & to serve him for subsidye in any other war, and in the meane tyme to enterteyne an opinion that he would in the end doe great matters for the common cause, under which shadow he hath well done his owne busines. Now he sees he must take off the masque and declare, and finding no aydes offered him (with which I doe beleeve he would undertake the war, for his spiritt is far above his meanes), that he resolves to make a peace advantagious to himselfe, and necessarye to make his new conquests profitable, and to save his honour with the world by a show & apparance & by casting the blame upon others, yet so that, by the reputation of his arming, which the Imperialls feare, he may procure by treatye the libertye of the sea, & the restitution of the Princes of Meckelburgh & the retirying of the Emperor's forces from these parts; all which con-

CAMD. SOC.   K

cerne his owne safety & interest, which if he cannot obteyne I doe beleeve he will make a brave & bold attempt, being sure of his retrayct, & knowing he shall make the better peace being in the field and armed. To which end he hath made provision of forty thousand last of corne and 1000 firery wagons, a new invention of war, & hath fitting and contracted for 300 ships & vessels to transport his men, victualls, & munition to Stralsond. And, howsoever he may in the meane tyme enterteyne a treatye, I am of opinion he will not conclude it untill he have landed there; first, because he cannot licence his horse safely so neare his new lands without entyre satisfaction; and that, having appeared within the lists and openly offered himselfe upon the place, if he find no such solid aydes as he doth require, he may retyre, *son honneur à couvert*, and defend himself from any objection; but that he wilbe far engaged without supply is not in my creede, for he is the king of the world now that best knowes and does his owne busines.

To these circumstances I may add, that the King hath publicquely professed that he will make no peace untill he hath drawne his sword in Germanye and spoke one word for the Prince Elector Palatine, for that was his owne phrase, and it is sayd here that the stay of the levies of Coll. Kniphusen, which were made in the eyes of the Emperor, was done only to disguise his ententions & to give the enemye hope of accomodation, & consequently not to bee too vigilant in preparations, but that underhand ther were new orders sent out to make less noyse; & we see he doth take upon him the troopes of the Elector of Brandeburg and Dansicke dismissed, to the number of 4000, and fills up all his Dutch regiments here. Lastly, the Chancelor doth begin to treate candidly with the Dansickers and to compleate the truce with Poland, as if they were desirous of peace & to have no impediment from these parts. All these I consider may be arts and gallant boutados, and I trust not in them, for here is somewhat to doe for the Kings revenew, for which they must nourish a good opinion that they will employ it well. But I will conclude that I am confident he will attempt somewhat, and take and leave as the wayes are easy or difficult, and according to such aydes as shalbe presented, and that he will treate in the field *l'espée à la main*, to come off with more honour among his enemies & defence of himselfe toward his friends.

This being the estate of this affayre, as far as I can collect, his Matie may worke and apply these counsells to the present treatyes in other parts in case of necessitye of war, to apprehend the oportunitye, and to take this martiall prince at the first bound in Pomerland, & to engage him bravely, whose declaration, reputation, & conduct will give new life to the good cause, and, if it must be peace, that it may be treated in conformetye & with common counsells, which will advantage all parts. For myselfe I have no power to goe farther, but I will use all my witts & sinews not only to keepe him in hope, but to settle him a revenew that wilbe equall to a good contribution upon the trades, which wilbe easely borne, & among many insensibly, & without which the trade it selfe would be more burthened or shutt up.

This letter hath already exceeded the proposed limitts, but, seing I doe only propose and relate which is my dutye, your Lordships benignetye will call the presumption zeale to his Maties and the publicque service, and continew me the grace & sanctuarye of your protection, as in his I humbly desire God to keepe your Lordship.

    · Your Lordship's most humble servant,
             Tho. Roe.

Part of the substance of this letter that concerneth the purpose of the King of Swede I have written to the King of Bohemia, not knowing his Matie hath any minister at the Haghe, the ambassador being as I heare gone for Bruxells & Mr. Carleton for England, neyther have I received one letter but from Mr. Carleton.

Elbing, 24 Jan. 1629, s.v.

On Feb. $\frac{6}{16}$ Roe wrote to Dorchester, still dating from Elbing, that Oxenstjerna had written to the King to allow him to disband some of his horse in Prussia, "lamenting the misery of the country, not able to feed them, and want of money to contain them in any discipline, to which, as I am secretly informed, he received a sharp answer that he should follow his instructions and not meddle nor trouble himself with the King's designs until he were called, but attend his government and use all his wits to keep the troops whole, and to find them means to subsist until the spring, and to leave the rest of the care to dispose and pay them to his Majesty. The Chancellor told me that he had order to recruit all the regiments here, and not to reform any. He daily takes on new and treats with those colonels that are licensed in Poland. So that he enters into infinite charge, and will have in these parts, besides his Swedes and his new levies in Germany, 17,000 foot and 5,000 horse, whose officers have order to be ready to march in April. His whole army, being drawn together, will consist of 30,000 foot and 8,000 horse for the field, leaving good garrisons in Prussia, Livonia, and his new lands. Provision, munition, victuals, and a fleet are making ready in Sweden to transport and attend the King, and they deny not that this preparation is made for Pomerland."

XXIII. *Sir Thomas Roe to Sir Robert Anstruther.*

MY VERY GOOD LORD,

State Papers,
Poland.
Feb. $\frac{7}{17}$,
1629-30.

I have received two letters from your Lordship since I wrote to you and by them perceive the safe arrivall of all myne, to those of the 8 Jan. Since I have borne a great adventure, having written of the 14 Jan. to my Lord of Dorchester, enclosed by Mr. Gordon to you and to the King of Bohemia of the 21 Jan. in a cover to Sig^{re} Marco Calendrino, to be delivered to your Lordship, and my last of the 26 Jan. to yourselfe, with another for England, with a flying seale, that you might see my thoughts of the present estate of affayres here, and know the grounds and hopes conceived of the passage of the King of Swede into Germanye. I shalbe most glad to heare that all those are safely come to you, and then I shall thinke the danger past, or if any have miscarried to know which it is, that I may supply the matter. Judging nothing more requisite to his Maties service then a clear knowledge of the proceedings and dessignes of this King and what use might be made of his virtue, by communication of counsells, eyther for war or treaty of peace, I have continued to enforme my Lord of Dorchester of all circumstances and passages, that your master may make his own judgement, and to poynt out such rocks and hinderances as may divert the purpose of war, which wee foresee in great preparations, and to show the opportunityes and advantages which may be apprehended to the good cause if God inspire us to know the season, which is a high poynt of wisedome. And therefore I will pronounce to your Lordship that I am confident the tyme wilbe offered, and that this brave king will appeare *districto gladio* in Pomerland, and take or leave, as he sees occasion, favour or admonish him, or that his friends come to him or forsake him. Therfore, if the publicque neede his ayd (which I feare it doth more then a trust in a Spanish treatye), lett him be taken at his own bound. It is our duty to watch and explore. I beseech your Lordship joyne with me to persuade in England and Hollande to embrace this opportunitye to consider it and weigh it, at least if the reede of our treatyes[a] fayle us; for, if it be overslipt, I have discharged my duty and conscience; he will make his peace not only with the Emperor, but perhaps with the Catholicque League, which hath beene proposed to him, and enjoy glorye and profitt enough in his new conquests, having forced the Emperor to stoope to conditions good for himselfe, and so he will rest, and never hope more nor thinke of us, who did not *prospicere rebus nostris* while it was yet to-day. Now is the tyme, which if we lett escape will never returne to us from Swede; for, though the king may keepe a bodye and forme of militia, yet he will lincense his horse and ease himselfe of his great charge, and goe home and gett children, to make war that way against the posterity of the King of Poland, which all his nobilitye desire. Now he is armed, his bloud warme, the expence of leavies borne, his soldiers veterans, *ad oram Rubiconis*, yet he is so wise a prince that he will not pass over unless his friends build the bridge. He may make a gallant attempt and bravado, but he will never be engaged *sine fundo* in all tempests *ubi jacere anchoras*. A sudden prosperity may entice him beyond his first ends, which are his owne safety, and spinne out a

---

[a] *i.e.* the negotiations with Spain.

naturall ambition, but it were not providence in us to trust so great a game to fortune. Therefore, my Lord, doe what you thincke is fitting for his Maties service, and, if you will make me the author of this instigation, send the coppy of my letter freely. I am content not only to avow what I write and to adventure any censure, but to be an holocaust for my King and that distressed cause which can never revive but by the union of our master and Swede with Holland. To ease myselfe and to assure the confidence I repose in your Lordship's judgement and favour to me, I send you also this with *cachet volant*, that you may digest and apply my grounds where you find they may be profitable.

And because there are many things which seeme to oppose the dessigne of the King of Swede, especially jealousyes, perhaps sowed by the enemye, and perhaps taken up as a subterfuge, yet it is our part to remove all and to plane and prepare the way as smooth as we are able, at least to provide to ourselves this comfort, not to have fayled by our owne negligence. And therfore to your Lordship I will further ad an increase of jealousye of the King of Denmark; a poynt I have formerly touched in my other letters, and wherein you may exercise your prudence that it take not roote, and use the advice so tenderly that it nourish not, nor kindle a sparke that easely flameth. I saw a letter to the Chancellor of Swede that one Enhuse, a man favored of the King and Prince of Denmarke, and Coll. Hulke, had both taken service of Wallenstein, and a coppy of his letter to that king, that he accepted them *in gratiam regni, Regisque Daniæ*, and that he had chosen Hulke to putt in garrison in Newstatt, hearing of the great preparations of the King of Swede, as one in whom his Matie had mutuall confidence. This correspondence is scandalous, and I beseech your Lordship penetrate into it; ease us of the feare, and apply such remedies both from England and from your owne authority in that court, where you have so much knowledge, as may take away all stumbling, offence, or doubt of diversion on that syde, and all suspition, the stepmother of good accord, on this.

SIR THOMAS ROE'S MISSION.   71

I will propose one consideration more. By the sparkling of these jealousies I have discovered an emulation, naturall to so neare neighborhood, betweene these two brave Kings of Denmark & Swede, who should both be deare to us, *multis nominibus*, and nourished in mutuall confidence and friendship. But I foresee some seedes that may fall into too fruitfull earth, and bring forth dissention betweene them, so malicious is the divell, if the wisedome of his Matie prevent it not, and I know no so safe and profitable way as by a stricter league among ourselves and employment of the King of Swede elsewhere to the common ends; wherein the King of Denmark shall reape part of the securitye and profitt, perhaps, for greatnes of stomack, against his will. But I enter too deepe into future matters, though I know this to be no panique and vague feare, and will conclude that, howsoever my zeale may transport me, the soule of wisdome is foresight and prevention, and my master shall not only have comfort but honor in moderating the ill humours of the world and disposing them to his owne and the publique service, which God prosper to him and him to his church; to whose gratious keeping I committ your Lordship. Resting,

                                                Etc.

Elbing, $\frac{7}{17}$ Feb^r, $\frac{1629}{1630}$.

XXIV. *Sir Thomas Roe to Frederick, titular King of Bohemia.*

MAY IT PLEASE YOUR MA^{tie},

I wrote your Matie a very large letter of the 21 Jan. directed to Sig^{re} Marco Calandrini in Hamburg, wherein I presumed not only to give you account of my labours in these parts, but what I could collect of the dessignes of the King of Swede to pass into Pomerland or to make peace with the Emperor, and my humble opinion how to apply his resolutions to your Maties service. I have nothing to recant in that letter; for, though I know what the practices for peace are, and from whom they move, yet I see the preparations

State Papers,
Poland.
Feb. $\frac{14}{25}$,
1629-30.

against it increase, and doe constantly beleeve that an occasion wilbe offered, if God inspire those that neede it, to apprehend it.

Monsieur Charnacé, the French ambassador, being in his way home as far as Denmark, mett there with new letters and orders to returne to the King of Swede, which he instantly did. Nothing is discovered of his instructions but that it is beleeved he hath received larger commission to give some assurance of contribution, or to negotiate a confederacye; and, though this king seeme not to trust in the French, yet we hope it may keepe him from precipitation. God send the one constancye and the other prosperitye.

Colonell Kniphaussen, returned also into Swede, brought better assurance of good affections in the King of Denmark, which hath much eased one care; and, howsoever it may be act of eyther syde, it is a necessary care to preserve a good understanding betweene those crownes, of which there is more neede then is fitt for me to write; but your Matie will receive more certeyne enformation from Sir Robert Anstruther, into whose province it were presumption in me to enter.

Fresh troopes dayly arrive in Swede, and I am confident that the king will not be the first to conclude peace untill he hath drawne his sword on the place and offered himselfe to the generall cause, which oportunitye, if it be overslipt, will never return from Swede; but he will carry peace in tryumph, grounded upon his owne reputation and the feare of the enemie, which is a solid foundation.

Here have beene (returning from the Elector of Brandeburgh) ambassadors of the Duke of Pomerland with the prince. They negotiated a meanes to make peace, both fearing to have their countryes made *sedes belli.* With the Chancellor of Swede they only made enquiries and discoveries what were the King's intents, but I thincke they advanced nothing anywhere but to know here was no power to enterteyne or declare any thing.

I cannot perceive that the Elector hath taken any resolution nor made any appoyntment with the King, but that now, returning to the marquisate, he doth depend on a convention with the Duke of

Saxe, according to whose counsells he may eyther declare or must suffer patiently, for, though in effect his countrye is lost, yet he is loth to see the King of Swede land in Pomeran, to give occasion to the Emperor to lodge upon him and to have his owne house first pulled downe, to stay the generall fire. Such is the case, that it is hard to judge whither the medicine or disease be most dangerous; it is like cutting for the stone, and doth require a brave courage to resolve to buy ease at the perill of life. The next weeke I shall meete his Highness at Marienburg, where I will doe as God shall inspire me, for I have no direction. The hope of all my intentions being thus squared, that if it be requisite to treate peace, that it may be generall for Germany and all the princes and religion oppressed together, which may be hoped, if the severall treatyes of his Matie and the States and the King of Swede were joyned and carried with common counsells and ends. But if their ministers shall discover that falshood (which it is honest to feare), that these treatyes of the house of Austria be only to seperate friends and to rocke occasion asleepe, whose eyes should ever be waking, that then by a well formed and grounded union war may be declared, denounced, and made together. So whither the election shalbe peace or war, if those three were first strictly colleagued, eyther might be undertaken with more securitye and foundation, and the lesser princes might refuge under that shadow with more assurance, and in the worst event it wilbe safer and more honor to strive and struggle then to lye downe. And the enterteyning of a treaty by the King of Swede should not make others negligent: for honor will bring him into the field, if but to seeme to invite those that perhaps he thinks will not come, and there is the subject of wisedome to take tyme, and I am constant if a league be offered him from us and Holland that he will take it. Howsoever it is a base and abject estate to despayre, and therefore while there is one star shining your Matie will give me leave to hope and to endeavour, which is the office of a man, and leave the judgement to God. I will presume to ad one word more: this King hath solemnly protested that he will not depose armes untill he hath spoken one word for your Matie in Germanye (that was his own phrase), and glorye will contend with policye in this resolution, for he hath unlimited thoughts and is the likelyest instrument for God to worke by in Europe. We have often observed great alterations to follow great spiritts, as if they were fitted for the tymes, certeynly *ambit fortunam Cæsaris:* he thinks the ship cannot sinke that carries him and doth thus oblige prosperitye. If he deceive me, I feare he will have to good an excuse against his accusers, and I had rather be deceived in him then by ourselves, for there is no greater comfort in adversitye then not to fayle ourselves. If I knew not your Maties benignitye, I would not use this libertye: but, having no other way to employ my talent, I presume to write my thoughts both to my owne master and to you and then, as I ought to submitt them. I know not how the treaties in England and Holland proceede; but, being desired by the Baron Zierotin (who constantly professeth his service to your Matie) to move you that if there be any meanes in a generall treatye to deliver him from banishment and adversitye that you will vouchsafe to remember his sufferings, being resolved to seeke no other way but by your Matie, I have done the office which I promised, not doubting your owne wisedome and goodnes best knowes what is fitt and possible to be done for him. I humbly aske leave to kiss her Maties hands; and this first fault to omitt to write I hope she will pardon in him that prayes for both your Maties with the devout heart of

       Your Maties most humble servant,
              THO. ROE.

Elbing, 16/26 Feb. 1628.

On Feb. 26 / March 7 Roe wrote to Dorchester from Danzig: "I have finally taken my leave of the Chancellor of Sweden, who hath used me honourably, and, by letters, of the King. I have yet nothing to recant of my former . . . concerning his preparations and designs. I know well he entertains a treaty with the Emperor, but on conditions so gallant and advantageous to him and his friends, and so difficult to be obtained of the Emperor, . . . and that I see daily new forces raised and a diligence to take on all that can be gotten by the disarming in Poland, Prussia, and Danzig, wherein the Imperials also labour for their part; yet I cannot believe he would cast away so great a charge without a full resolution to do somewhat, especially seeing I know he hath also taken time to resolve to the 20 April, expecting to hear the resolution of other princes, as his Majesty, the French, and the Lords the States; for accordingly he will either make war or peace : and this is a noble and brave proceeding, both with his friends and enemies, and if the opportunity be lost, as we must never expect the like occasion; so I have just cause to fear that he may fall into another quarrel, which I know would much discontent his Majesty, and were very pernicious to the public. The cause is tender, and I dare not touch it roughly; but I have discovered great ambition in that King, and that he aimeth at, above all things, to be Lord of that whole sea as well of the gates as of the storehouse and chambers,[a] and the least spark would kindle a fire between him and the King of Denmark, who I justly fear will give him cause as being either too envious or too imperial. This language his Majesty will vouchsafe to pardon me, for I am very privately advised, and from a hand of credit that knows it, that the King of Denmark, disliking the interposition of the King of Sweden in matters of Germany, sent privately to persuade the Duke of Pomerland to deliver the Isle of Rügen into his protection, which if he would do he would secure him from the landing of the King of Sweden, and that he would send all his ships to defend the coast, knowing that the other durst not attempt in the main,[b] if that island were kept and harbour given in it for his shipping. But the Duke of Pomerland utterly refused; whereupon Wallenstein despatched to Colonel Hatzfeld to work the Duke to consent, which shows too great and too secret an intelligence between them, and I know, if this practice were revealed to the King of Sweden, that he would revenge it, for he wants only occasion; and therefore his Majesty may both make good use of the intelligence to the King of Denmark, and will be pleased to take care of any breach between them, which would be mortal to the affairs in Germany, and ruin all trade in this sea, wherein the King of Sweden is grown already too great, and there is more cause to balance than to increase him."

XXV. Elizabeth, titular Queen of Bohemia, to Sir Thomas Roe.

HONEST THOM,

Your letter was verie welcome to me, for I ame glade you are well in Barbarie, though I wish you in the same kinde here.[c] The King will tell you himself how much he esteems both you and your advertisements, which are indeed verie good, and, if the King of Sweden gett the Emperour to restore the Duke of Meckebourg, I

State Papers,
Poland.
March $\frac{5}{15}$,
1629-30.

---

[a] "storehouse and chambers" interlined in Roe's hand; deciphered "ports" in another copy.
[b] *i.e.* On the main land.   [c] *i.e.* As ambassador here.

know what both we and you, I belleeve, shall think. Sir Henry Vane is still heere and not like to stirr so soone: he carieth himself veric well, and is as little confident of the treaties with Spaine as we are, though by Dudlie Carleton, who is everie day expected heere out of England, we shall heere great matters from thence: when he comes I will lett you know what it is. The speech heere of truce is not so much as it was: all things in England are the same, without anie great change. The Queene my sister lookes to be brought to bed in June, and my brother is at Newmarquet. The King heere hath beene evill first of a sore throat and since of a weakness which took away his stomack, but after that an impostume or two broke out uppon his bodie he is well againe and I hope will be abroad at Easter: he was never so evill as he kept his bed with. The phisitians say that his desease is come from the misfortune he had last yeare in the water; indeed he was never well since; but I hope all is past. I write this to you because I know you will heare manie rumours of his sickness that may make you afrayed, and I ame sure you will be glade to heere he is so well, for I know and ame sure of your love to us. I hope at your returne you will come this way, which I shall be verie glade of. I dare speake more to you then write, and for your letters lett me ever know what I shall doe with them to shew them to this ambassadour or not and you may be confident I will, for I assure you that nothing shall ever make me other then

Your constant friend,

ELIZABETH.

I pray send me word if you have receaved the letter I writt you by Macquay. I shall wish you heere one Monday for to see a comedie, the Scornfull Ladie, acted by your cosen Honywood and some other of our countremen, to passe the time a little to the King.

The Hagh, this $\frac{A}{5}$ of Marche.

XXVI. Sir Thomas Roe to Sir Robert Anstruther.

MY HONORABLE LORD,

I have received your letters of the 3 and 4 present, being glad that all myne to that time have found safe passage. Since I have written you the dates in the margen. I infinitely thanke your Lordship for so much paynes taken to cleare and ease me in the objections and doubts infused to me of ill understanding betweene those princes whose prosperitye we both desire, and I wish it may prove as we desire. But you will find by a passage of my later letters that, though this Chancelor perhaps know no more then he opened to me, yet I have knowne of some offers made (and that is all I dare write without a cyphar) which both show a resolved disaffection and would have made an open quarrell. But God, that otherwise disposed that dessigne, will, I hope, inspire both their hearts to know *unam esse viam agros eorum per longum tempus possidendi: firmè inter se invicem pacem et concordiam colere,* which was the counsell of Epaminondas to the emulous republicques of Greece.

Our discourse of this King hath a tertian fever. One day brings matter of confidence, the next of doubt. The preparations of the armye are constant, and the Secretary Grobb, newly arrived out of Swede, hath brought orders for mony now given out to all the regiments for their recrews; on the other syde, the comming hither of the Baron de Dona from the Emperor to treate (of which I enformed you the last weeke) is confirmed, merchants having received orders to provide mony for him; and Mr. Sanderson, whom I credited as a secretarye to resyde in that Court, hath written hither, that, though the provisions for war goe on, yet that the resolution of passing the sea doth depend of the actions of Sir Francis Cottington in Spayne. These are the two particulars which most trouble me, that the treatye is brought home to the dore of the King of Swede, and the pre-

State Papers
Poland.
March ,
1628.

text of it home to us, that, seeing we doe no good, we may beare the shame of diverting others from doing it, occasion of which scandall may be taken from want of communication, though such is his Maties wisedome and integritye to the good cause that we deserve it not.

For my selfe I have done my dutye according as God hath inspired me, and, as I beleeve, was requisite to his Maties service, not out of any spirit of contention or opinion of my owne judgement, but as a part of my function to looke out, and watch, and say, I see a troope comming, and his marching is furious like Jehu, and perhaps the Lord hath sent him; submitting both my reasons and affections to my master and superiors, and therefore whosoever shall take offence I shall not feare the worst can be done to me. I feele already the want of mony. In the rest I am a true subject, and pittye their impotencye who cannot beare truth. Herein I trust the goodnes and magnanimitye of my master, knowing well that in all great consultations some truths, though in themselves admittable, are not alway alike received unless they meete with abondant generositye, such as is in him to whom an honest man may alway speake truth and open and discharge his conscience, which is a great happines for us servants, and will make him the wisest prince in the world; hearing, being the organ of all knowledge and judgement, if it fall out otherwise, though some politicians have called prosperous wickednes a virtue, yet I never heard of any so *effronté* as to say improsperous virtue was wickednes, and of Sertorius, who was a rebell, the worst censure was that he was *vir calamatosæ virtutis*. You see, my Lord, I have little to doe when I fall to play with words, and to dare Fortune, whom the weakenes of men made a weaker god. I will then conclude, letting your Lordship know that I have gotten a ship, and hope to sett sayle within 10 dayes to such ports as your letters shall direct me, at least if I can procure to touch at Lubecke, being bound for the Sond; but if I must goe thither I shall find meanes to transport myselfe according to occasion or your Lordship's commands, whom I pray God to keepe, and your noble Lady, and all your famelye, in health and honour, and to the joy of

    Your Lordship's most humble and affect. servant.

Dansicke, $\frac{19}{16}$ March $\frac{1629}{1630}$.

[*Indorsed*] To Sir Rob. Anstruther, 19 Mar. 1629.

XXVIII. Sir Thomas Roe to Sir Robert Anstruther.

MY NOBLE LORD,

 All my carriage being aboard I lye here wynd bound, and expect every howcr to be called away; passage to Lubecke I cannot gett, so that I take what I can for the Sond, where I beseech you that your help and counsell may meet me. I thanke you with a true heart for all the favours I have received from you, particularly for your last, that brought me letters from princes whom I honour, and for whose prosperitye I would spend that worst and last part of my life not worth the living. Good manners requires an answere, but I will entreat you to excuse me; what I could write I take no pleasure in, and I remember that David did conjecture of good newes because Ahimaaz brought it, who was a good man; but I have none to relate; let Cushi tell the rest. The Baron of Donau is here arrived with a seasonable trayne and is confident of peace; his enterteynment by the common people was little grateful, calling him openly and ironically the reformer and saviour of men's soules, for he is the persecutor of our religion, and the executioner of the tirannicall decrees agaynst the professors in Silesia. Here are dayly expected ambassadors from the King of Denmark, the Electors of Saxe and Brandeburgh as mediators, and shortly at Elbing from the King of Swede. Excellent friends; and I will leave them the same blessing which Cardinall Caraffa gave the gaping people of Paris when the holy father did unbind them from a generall inter-

State Papers, Poland. April $\frac{4}{15}$, 1630

diction and absolved them of all their sinns: *quis non crederit;* for
when they flocked for the benefitt of a pardon he pronounced
Quandoquidem hic populus vult decipi, decipatur;[a] yet there is no
preparation for the war in apparance diminished. So that I hope
more of the King of Swede's owne person then of all his countrye,
for he is both *caput* and *cor regni;* he is all, and worth all, and we
could not have left him without our owne help, and so are become
wittily and industriously miserable. My Lord, you see my freedome with you. I will neyther write for England nor the Haghe,
if you please to let them know why, I leave it to your discretion;
and if you send my letter I care not, for I am so afflicted that
nothing can add to it, being able to write nothing fitt to be read,
and having received nothing at all from whence I expected, or of
that little I have it had beene an happines to be ignorant. And so
the good God bless our King and keep your Lordship in his sacred
safetye.

Your Lordship's true humble servant.

Dansicke, $\frac{6}{16}$ Apr. 1630.

XXVIII. Sir Thomas Roe to Frederick, titular King of Bohemia.

MAY IT PLEASE YOUR Ma[tie],

I have received your Ma[ties] letters of the 6 March, being glad
that myne of January were safely arrived in these jealous tymes;
others I adventured of the 15 Feb. which I hope have had as good
success. I left Prussia on the 16 of this moneth and arrived here
the 19, desirous to have found the King of Denemarke to have
finished my service; but he is in Holstein, and his removes are so
uncerteyne that I cannot resolve whether to attend or seeke him;
but a Parlament being here summoned within three weekes (in
which it is thought the Lady Christienne shall come to tryall), I
shalbe most sure to have leysure to wayt upon him. In the meane
tyme, and not knowing whether I shall returne by Holland, the

[a] *Sic.*

whole sea being beleaguered with the vermyne of Dunkercque, I will presume to enforme your Matie in what estate, at least in my judgment, I left the affayres of the King of Swede, and the preparations eyther to war or a treatye. The Baron of Donau, President of Silesia, arrived in Dansicke the 19 April, new stile, the day, as he pretended, of the appoynted convention of commissioners from the Swede and ambassadors from the King of Denmark to mediate and treate a peace, whose not appearing he seemed to take in ill part, yet hath patience enough to wayt for them. His comming and some practise in the cittye hath raysed a suspition that the Emperor hath intelligence among them which hath caused them to double their guards and to suspend the licensing of their soldiers, for they feare if the peace ensue not that the Imperialls will prevent the Swede and march into Prussia, or their territorye, to make it the seate of the war. But I thinke these are pannicque and burghers' feares, grounded on no reason, for we see that Wallenstein's orders in Pomeran make all provision for defence, and to contract his forces into the strengths and passes of that countrye and Markeland. The preparations both in Swede and Prussia proceed in the same measure both by taking on men and hyring ships, but the continuance of this charge doth not secure me, for if the King of Swede purpose peace he shall yet gayne his expense by show of war, and may with more ease beare an extraordinarye a few moneths then the war many, and therefore I feare we see the best syde.

Yet all the officers are of opinion that the King doth only temporise and meet the Emperor in his owne arts, and that they rather strive who shall prevayle by witt to steale one from the other an oportunitye then with a mind to depose armes. And there is much to make us beleeve it on the Swede's part (in the other it is habituall), because, as he will treate so he does proceed in action, for lately his garrison in Stralsond hath invaded and taken Rugen and driven the Imperialls into a corner, where, though they are fortefyed, they cannot long hold out. This island I know was the principall marke and ground of the King of Swede to pass into Pomeran, both

CAMD. SOC.   M

for his retraict and a safe station for all his fleete, munition, and
provision, of which being possessed he is secure and wilbe greatly
encouraged, and nothing doth more make me hope then that he
hath begun prosperously there, and this newes hath extreamely
altered the Baron Donau. The Chancellor of Swede, upon his
arrival, removed further off to muster his army: and there hath
beene none scene yet from Denmarke, and this also doth much
assayle his patience. Lieutenant Colonell Ruthen arrived from
Swede at Dansicke since the comming of Donau, and reports that
the King had sent an expresse to his Matie to know his resolution
what help he might expect, and had answere none; but I beleeve it
not, or else it is the same given Sir James Spence; for, seeing the
delayes of Spayne, it is impossible that this occasion should be
neglected or contemned.

He reports that Monsieur Charnacé, the French ambassador, being
returned to the King of Swede, offered and brought creditt and
effects for 200,000 dollars for a contribution, to be continued yearly;
but the King, having no other ayd from other parts, refused it; yet
proposed that if his Matie would double it and give valuable assignations for payment and continue it untill the end of the war and
make no peace in Italye *nisi communicatis consiliis*, that he would
breake off all treatye, and proceed in his dessignes, the answere of
which yet depends. If this be true, what a miserye it is to lose
such an oportunitye, the terror, armes, conduct, reputation, and
prosperitye of so brave a king and capteyne, lett those that flatter
themselves judge, for a summe so contemptible, or the world must
judge us blinded with perverse counsells or blasted with a ruynous
fate; for if that summe would content him (which I ever judged
and collected) it would make no difference from whose hands or
from how many it were contributed; but, being able to doe nothing,
I have yet sent to the Chancellor my last documents, rather to show
my zeale and to discharge my conscience then in hope that words
will make war: concluding that if a peace succeeds that not only the
fayrest occasion that I have seene in all the war is given up, but

we ourselves, that most neede it, have not beene the least accessories.
I send your Matie the coppyes of my last letters to him; wherein
you may find some advertisements that are not current; but such
as I received them I made the best use of I was able; and now,
having more leysure to praye, I refer the resolution to God, who
only knowing the hearts of princes will direct them as his instruments to his owne purposes, which are blessed in the end; to whose
gratious keeping I devoutly commend your Matie, and rest
                Your Maties most humble unprofitable servant.
Elsenore, 18/28 Apr. 1630.

XXIX. *Sir Thomas Roe to Elizabeth, titular Queen of Bohemia.*

MAY IT PLEASE YOUR MA^tie,

I humbly kiss your Maties hands for your gratious letters, which State Papers,
comfort me that my zeale to your service hath as much operation Poland.
upon your goodnes as other mens prosperitye; and God knowes April 18/28, 1630.
what I would doe or suffer; neyther doe I doubt that every thing I
write is safe in your Maties handes, nor will I ever doe any thing
but what is honest to justefye, though sometyme it is not safe nor
wisedome to be exposed to envye. I will write your Matie no newes,
being assured you must be my interpreter to the King, to whome I
have written what I thinke usefull for his service, doeing the same
in substance for England, where how my freedome is interpreted
I know not, having in 6 moneths had no letter, order, nor answere,
nor mony since my departure, which is but an ill symptome.
Whatsoever you thinke may serve to publique ends your Matie may
freely communicate with Sir Hen. Vane or his Excellencye; but
where I write like Thom. Roe and breake out, that passion the
King may be pleased to smother. If Sir Henry Vane had eyther
order or purpose to correspond with me it was his turne to give me
occasion, but I thinke the divers natures of our employments imposed on us both a discreet silence. I am gotten thus far toward
home in a ship called the " King of Bohemia," and carrying his

picture in our coulors; but, not finding the King of Denmarke in this island, I must stay him and new order, for my old is stale and I know not how to use it, neyther am I sure what way I shall take from hence, the sea being full of Dunkercque harpyes, whom I would be loth to visitt. I should be infinitely glad to see your Matie, for at Rhenen I conteyned myselfe, but there is also some cause that I would not see Holland, which was made a bayt to send me to the North, where yet I have done his Matie honor and my country service, and effected all or more then was imposed on me: thus God doth bless his servants, and I will pray for your Matie while I have life and the honour to be knowne to be now

Your Maties most antient and most humble servant.

Elsenore, $\frac{28}{18}$ Apr. 1630.

After Roe's return, he heard of Gustavus's landing in Germany. "The landing," he wrote on Aug. 16th, 1630, to Mr. Sanderson, the English agent in Sweden, "of the King of Sweden in Germany (which few would believe here) hath raised him such a reputation that his Majesty hath taken it into serious consultation how to aid and supply him whose maintenance his own virtue hath endeared to us, and taught us to know how necessary he is to the general welfare and liberty of Christendom, as if he were elect of God for the great work. I should have returned to him, but upon more mature deliberation it was thought fit first to lay the foundation sure, and if he hold out this summer I am assured before the next spring his Majesty will send to him in such a fashion as shall be most acceptable. In the mean time we all pray for him; and you shall extremely value yourself with his Majesty if you do in a discreet manner and without obligation by intimation of these purposes encourage him, which I assure you are real, and, if I did not know it, for no advantage I would deceive that brave prince. Our treaty with Spain depends and is a secret to me, but that I believe the House of Austria will give up nothing they can hold for words nor without hard blows."

APPENDIX.

I. Instructions of Gustavus Adolphus to Sir James Spens.

State Papers, Sweden. Oct. [?] 1624.

Ane schort informatione gevine to Sir James Spens, Knyght, for helping his memorie to y̅ᵉ mor large explicatione off y̅ᵉ schort articles proposed concerning the league.

What the King's Majestie of Sweden judgethe and thinkethe of the reparatione of the decayed caus of religione and principallie of the restitutione of the King of Bohemia, the said Sir James Spens hathe sufficiently understood, being present, and by the conditions off the league annexit persaivethe how it behowethe the King of Sueden to be secured, and what he thinkethe necessary, and also willethe his confederates to doe to that end.

Bot this it pleased his Majestie hier to repeat, that ther ar only tuo wayes by whiche his Majestie iff he must be orderer [a] of the bissines must mak his way, the one by the Wessell [b] passing throche Poll[and] to Silesia, the wyther [c] by the Wiser. The first doethe most please becaus it semethe most neirly to concerne the weilfear of this Kingdome, neyther hes it so many and so gryt impedimentes to hender. It hethe only Dansik to lett, whiche, being maid frendlie by the intercessione of the confederat freindes and brocht to a mor sound mynd, or then by force compelled to obedience, will mak the remanent proceding free and saiff. The wyther semes to hawe gryte difficulties bothe becaus of the abundance of strong and mychte tounes and the neirnese in frendship of dyvers Lordes, whois territories must be past throche and themselffis offendit: bot iff this

---

[a] "director" written above.   [b] Vistula.   [c] *i.e.* other.

last shall be mor approwethe by his Majestie and confederates, as it is credible that it wilbe for divers respectes, the Kingis Majestie of Sueden, will willinglie accommodat yourselff to the desyres and counsells of the rest, and will indeworr to restor Germanie by passing throche Germanie, seing it pleasethe not the rest that he pass throche Poll[and]. And that this matter may be undertakine by sum sur maner and withe good hope, his Majestie shall, in favoure of his confyderates and the comon cause, bring to the feldes and sustayne upone his owne chargis tuelff regiments off foott and tuo thowsand horsmen, wnto whom it shalbe necessar that the rest of the confederates joyne four and twentie regimentes off foot and sex thowsand horse. Besydes his Majestie shall bring with him als mony piece of canone and ordinance with wyther sort off all kynd of munitione as shalbe needfull for his camp, except only the suldeoures armes, whiche everie on of the confederates salbe holdine to furnise *pro rata* according to his pairt, or then they shalbe bocht withe one monthes wadges in mancre as shalbe hierefter schawine: as for horse waggones and wictualles to the armie the rest of the confederates must prowyd them.

As for the charges of the war, in his Majesties judgment they must be so dewyded among the confederates that his Majestie shall tak upone him the third pairt, to witt, the pay of tuelff regimentes of foott and tuo thowsand horse, and whatsoever charges and expenses followethe them. Also the canon [a] and whatsoever is requyred unto them and all wyther kynd of munitione and ordinarie expenses whiche ar to be undergone for the exercise of the suldeoures, the defence of the camp in skarmises and battelles.

The Kinges Majestie of Gryt Brittane, and iff please him to joyne with him the generall esteates of the United Prowinces, shall sustayne the vyther third pairt off the burdine, to witt, the payment off 12 regimentes off foott and four thowsand horse, and the expenses for raising them. The rest of the confederat princes off Germanie and the tounes shall contribut so muche as may suffice to lifft and sustayne the wyther third part of the armie, consisting off 12 regimentes of foot and tuo thowsand horse, and shall provyd wagones and horses for the ordinance and ther instrumentes, puder and ball, as also neidfull wictuales for the

---

[a] "ordinance" written above.

arme; and so you shall supplie and mak out the third pairt of the charge.

The rest of the charge and expenses of the warr, to witt, the payment of generall officeres, the gryt quantitie of pulder and bullet, and wyther thinges whiche shalbe requyred in the longsum, and streatt beseeginges of gryt tounes and campes, shalbe devyded efter the samm maner among the said confederates, that on third pairt shalbe furnished by his Majestie, ane wyther third pairt by the Kinges Majestie of Gryt Bryttaine, and the resting third by the confederat princes and tounes.

Concerning the suldeours armes neidfull bothe to foott and horse, thei must be prepared and furnished efter the samm maner that everie on of the confederats prowyd all thinges for his ownne forces. Bot becaus it concernethe his Majestie abowe the rest, as being to be the leader off the armie, that all thinges may answer his disyr, and that nothing be vanting in the just tyme, and that the oportunitie of poorforming affaires be not lost, his Majestie estemes it fitt concerning the preparation of armes that everie on of the confederates shall delyver the armes for his pairt to the Kinges Majestie, iff they be in reddines; then (besyd the three mounthes wadges whiche must be givine beforhand) they shall ad and pay the fourt mounthes wadges and delyver it to him that shall hawe his Majesties power, to the intent that armes may be bocht in tyme; the whiche therefore (three monthes being past) may be deduced from the suldeoures wadges and rackoned in this payment, so that armes may be provyded for the suldeoures without extraordinaire charges or burding to the confederates. Above all it wer most to be wished that all they who grone under the yok of the house of Austria, having ther heartes rased and trusting in ther owne strenthe, durst be bold to profese ther names openlie and enter in this league, for perhapes therby ther suld be the lese labour and difficultie, bothe in lifting the suldeoures and in chasing the seat of the warr, and in proceeding; bot to him who shall mor exactlie ponder all thinges it is credible that many, being strikine and witholdine by the fear of the imminent and new perill, shall lurk so long till ane sufficient armie do sett foot in Germanie, unto the whiche they may safflie flie, and in the whiche they may rest secure of ther owne. Yet notwithstanding to help thos that ar ether unwilling, or who doethe not intreat and urge itt, is no less unjust then to involve friends unwillinglie in war, fear, and the evills that theron do follow. Nether certanlie culd it be excused from temeritie iff any suld tak war in hand not being requysed (altho upone a most holsome intentione) in the whiche he war[a] not to be helped, bot shortlie deserted of thos for whois caus it wer undertakine. Therfor iff the matter shalbe seriously done, thes thinges must be tymouslie forsein and provyded for:—The King of Bohemia, for whois restitutione this labour must cheiflie be undergone, shall without delay try and searce the myndes of his friendes in Germanie, that he may throchlie know and understand who of them doethe approwe or disprowe the league and how muche everie on of his friendes will contribut in comone, that therby it may be rychtlie discerned what and how muche may be expected from his freindes and what may be feared from the rest, and principallie that it may be knowne that the princes of Germanie and tounes will tak upone them the third pairt of the expenses ; and iff ther mycht be drawne to doe sumwhat mor, considering that yt concernethe them most, it wold be of greyte momente to the finishing of the war. When thes thinges shalbe certanlie resolved and understud, then a league is quyetlie to be maid with the princes and tounes of Germanie, whiche being maid and confirmed, the King of Gryt Brittane for the levying of the said twelf regimentes of foot and four thowsand horse, the princes and tounes of Germanie for 12 regimentes of foot and 2000 horse, shall delyver and contribute expenses requysett for liffting,[b] togidder with three mounthes pay, as also armes for the suldeoures or in place therof the fourte mounthes pay, that all may be innumerate and delyvered at the first of Marche the yeir next following, 1625, in his Majesties handes, or his who shall have power from him, without any diminutione, that the suldeores may be in tyme levyed and provyded of armes, and that his Majesties indevoures, labour, and expenses be not maid in vaine. The pay shall begine the first of May, for it will fall necessarie that in that mounthe the grytest charges be, and all thinges prepared. And when May, Jun, July, and August shalbe expyred, for the whiche that three mounthes pay and the armes shalbe gowine beforhand, then from the first of September lett the pay of that mounthe, and so furthe from mounthe to mounthe, be in reddines, untill the tyme that

[a] were.   [b] levying.

ane end be put to the war. Iff everie on of the confederates shall contribute efter this maner, his Majestie shall doo good will to hawe a full armie reddie in dew tyme. Bot iff this counsell be divulgat and the Emperor withe thos of that league doo oppose himselff to the levying publictlie of suldeoures in Germanie, it appearethe that the bissines must be undertakine efter this maner; to witt, that his Majestie hawe in reddinese aganst the last of May nixtocum[a] his 12 regimentes of foott and 2,000 horse, and joyne also to their 2,000 Germane horsemen, whiche he can hawe in reddines aganst the appointed day to be in his companie or armie. He shall also find the meanes to levie four foott regimentes of Germanes as iff it wer to his ownne proper use; also ther may be in the midtyme levyed in Brittanie four regimentes of foott and in France wyther four regimentes, whiche shall land at Gotheburghe in May, and joyne them selffis to the King's armie, that so in the same mounthe of May the armie may consist off four and twentie regimentes off foot and four thowsand horse; off whiche regimentes, on regiment off foot must be lefft with the navie, whiche must be ridged out in the Germane Sea to defend the Germane Cost, and avert all hostill invasione from the kingdome of Sweden out of the sea. His Majestie with the rest of his foot and horse shall saile throche the Baltik Sea, and (leving in his navie three regimentes of foot for the desente therof, and that Sweden in the meantyme may be free from the hostill attemptes off Polland, as also that the transportatione of all necessarie thinges from Sueden may remaine free and nowayes impeded) shall have ane armie prepared and present off twentie regimentes of footh and four thousand horse.

The Kings Majestie, therfor, of Gryt Bryttane, shall consider whidder this armie consisting off aucht and twentie thowsand men be stronge aneuthe to resist the force and invasione of the Cesarranes, and fitt as thinges offer and occasione fallethe out to pase fordvart untill the tyme that the rest of the regimentes may be supplied and the horsmen gathered, and the wyther princes and tounes of Germanie may, and doe openlye, cum and profese ther names; bot iff this armie in the beginning shalbe opposed by a stronge arme off the Empereur, so that it can not commodiouslie pase fordwart, yet notwithstanding no man of sound

[a] next to come.

judgment will deny bot that iff it bee rychtlie commandit it is powerfull aneuche to defend the cost and portes and to mak saiff acces unto the rest, untill ether it grow to ane just quantitie, or then be fortyfied [a] with ane wyther new armie, wherby it may commodiouslie marche aganst the enimie.

This also is necessare without whiche his Maj. can undertak nothing: to wit, that on portt may be open to his Maj. off the Baltik Sea in the cost of Germanie and ane wyther at the Veser,[b] for it is necessar that ther be a saife arryvell and a place where the suldeours may be landed, the armie ordered, and wherto everie on may reteir in saiftie, wher also the navie must ly at anker and attend. Iff this can not be obtined, it is easie to judge that the proceding will not onlie be difficill, bot impossibill; for first to open a way by force and armes is dangerous, bot that whiche cheiflie is to be considerit in this point is this, that the princes and cities which possese thes portes are friendes and may by no meanes be offendit; therfor, the King of Gryt Brittane and the King of Bohemia most indevour to draw into thear syd the Dooks of Mekilbrughe and the Bischope of Brem,[c] withe the cities of Lubec, Hamburghe, and Brem, as also the Count of Emden, and iff it be possibill they must obtayne from the Dook of Mekilbrughe with his favour and leawe that the port of Wismer[d] and toune may be open and patent to his Majestie his navie and armie. And from the rest that the portt off Brem, or sum wyther commodiouse toune, wold resave his Maj[esty] his navie and armie. Iff that can be obtayned a gryt difficultie is overcum; iff not, maine impedimentes will cast them selffes in the way off this erand that it can not commodiouslie be undertakine.

The difficultie also of schipping for carying and transporting the suldeoures from Sueden to Germanie cumes hier to be considerit, neyther is thear a more commodiouse remedie then that the Lordes the Estates Generall of the United Provinces do mowe ther citizens and subjectes to give to his Maj. the wse[e] of so manie of ther schipes as he shall haue neid of. And, seing the transportatione requyred gryt charges, that the rest of the confederates do equallie participate therof with his Maj., eache sustayning a third pairt.

[a] *i. e.* re-inforced.　　　[b] The Weser.
[c] Bremen.　　　[d] Wismar.　　　[e] use.

APPENDIX. 91

Besydes it is not only profitabill for manie respectes but absolutlie necessar that the confederates obtayne the free use of bothe the seas Baltik and Germanie, without whiche nothing can be undertakine with any fruit, neyther can ther be maid any sure or commodiouse communication of thinges; and this can not be performed without two navies. In the Baltik Sea his Maj[esty] shall haue his owne navie, which shall attend in sum port of Germanie and shall secur his Maj[esty] off his returne in his owne kingdome, iff so matters do fall. Off this his Maj. shall hawe a care that it be stronge aneuche bothe in number and goodnes of shippes and furnished with all furnitour off war necessar to resist and repell by the grace off God all violence whiche may be attempted aganst his Maj[esty] and confederates in the Baltik Sea. It is necessar that there be ane wyther navie in the Germane Sea, whiche may war under the commandment of his Maj. in name of the confederates. For this use his Maj. hes now in reddinese anocht[a] war shippes in the port of Gothobrughe. Iff the rest of the confederates and cheiflie the King of Gryt Brittane will ether extraordinarlie furnishe money for bying sextein war schipes, or esteim it fitter that some diminutione be maid of the number of the suldeours, and that money be converted to the making up of that navie, thear may be ane brave navie prepared, whiche may conserve the use of that sea to the confederates and may not mak free intercours betwix Sueden and Germanie, that nothing be wanting ether to the sustayning or to the suplying the necessities and wants of the armie from Sueden, Brittane, France, the Netherlands, etc. The expenses of this navie and charges as weill in preparing it as in mentayning itt shalbe devyded amonge the confederates as the rest.

Sir James Spens must have a cair to understand betyme iff thes thinges be approved by the King of Gryt Brittane; and, iff thei please him, he mvst tak cair that the money for bying the schipes be in reddinese and delyverit unto the Commissioners of his Maj. when he cummethe, who shalbe peculiarlie appointed for that erand; whidder it be that his Maj. of Gryt Brittane will give the said money extraordinarilie for bying of the schipes or will deduce itt from the number of the suldeoures. It is requisit also that this may be maid quiklie knowne to his Maj[esty] that he may caus carie his ordinance for his shipping to Gothobrughe whill

[a] enough.

now the lackes and vateres are frosene with us; iff also it may be obtayned of the King off Gryt Bryttane that he wold furnishe to the navie a certaine number of irone ordnance it wold be off gryt moment to hestein and forder the preparation of the navie.

Morover Sir James Spens must sollicit and procur from the King of Gryt Bryttane that all Inglise and Scottes sayling throche the Baltik Sea and speciallie tovardes Dansik be prohibited to serwe the King of Poll. or any wyther (other) aganst the King of Sweden, and that they bring not any schip having ordinance too the portes of Spruce, and speciallie off Dansik, Elving, and Queinbrughe,[a] and that the King off Bohemia with the King of Gryt Bryttanes help obtayne of the Generall Esteates that no Holland schipes with ordinance seall to the said portes, muche lesse that they serve the King of Poll[and] or any wyther aganst the kingdome of Sweden, and bothe Inglishe, Scottes, and Netherlanders be prohibited to gowe them selffis in Warsaw to serwe the Poll or any wyther prince to the prejudice off the King of Sweden so long as his Maj[esty] is holdine bissied in this expedition.

Whatsoever of thes thinges shall pleas his Maj[esty] and shalbe approved by the rest of the Confederates it is necessar that with all diligence it be wrettine over hither, and the ambassadours from the Confederates cum to his Maj[esty] with pover to defyne and conclud.

This is word be word translated out of the Latine so nere as I culd.

II. GUSTAVUS ADOLPHUS TO SIR JAMES SPENS.

State Papers, Sweden.
Mar. 4/14, 1624.

Gustavus Adolphus, D. G. gratiam et favorem nostrum singularem Magnifice nobis sincerè dilecte et fidelis. Redditæ nobis sunt biduo abhinc literæ tuæ datæ 21 Januarii ex quibus intelleximus te junctis consiliis rationem restituendi rem communem à nobis propositam, Regi Britanniæ ac Principi Walliæ aperuisse. Hos quoque studium nostrum de re communi bene merendi gratum habuisse, et ut nobis totius rei directio committeretur, et ut Rex Britanniæ tertiam onerum

[a] Konigsburg.

partem sustineret, consensisse, adjectis quibusdam clausulis, denique diem 30mo Aprilis et Hagam comitis conventus legatorum, per quos de fœdere ac toto negotio statueretur, constituisse, ob quam causam tu nobis autor es, ut nostrum isthuc Legatum mittamus, conditionesque ita moderemur, ne earum difficultate, onerumque gravitate pressi ac deterriti fœderati se subtrahant, quemadmodum hoc uberius literis tuis explicantur. Ut autem et mentem nostram, et quid te facere velimus, intelligas, scias optamus, nos temporis angustia, quo minus Legatum aliquem huic mittamus excludi, et si nobis sat temporis esset, pregnantibus rationibus abstineri, itinerum difficultas hoc anni tempore tibi nota est, sive terra, sive mari eundum sit. Quominus autem ista ablegatio nobis placeat, primo obstat communis per orbem de hoc fœdere volitans fama, noxia cœptis ausisque nostris, quæ misso legato, etiam quocunque sub pretextu, non premetur, sed magis adaugebitur; quæ quidem non adeo magni æstimandi esset, si de voluntate et deliberato proposito Regis Britanniæ, cœterorumque fœderatorum certi essemus. At si quid interveniat, ut facile intervenire posse intelligimus, quod hoc consilium vel mutet, vel interturbet, detrahet isthæc mutatio et aliquid nomini nostro, si id nimium affectasse videamur; Idque ut magis metuamus, facit hæc inopinata ac insolita præparatio bellica à Rege Daniæ instituta, quæ si pro salute cunctorum est suscepta, est certe quod ceteris gratulemur, ac nobis ipsis, quod isto onere liberati simus. Aut si eo directa, ut hos conatus nostros impediat, haud putamus æquum, nos tantæ tamque periculosæ causæ obtrudere, aut ingerere, nisi cæteris nos avide invitantibus sollicitantibusque. Præter cetera vero id considerandum est, quod tibi presenti sæpius diximus, tanti momenti negotium hoc esse respectu nostri, ut conclusio ejus fidei ac industriæ alicujus Legati committi non possit. Si enim de subsidio pecuniario, aut mittendo milite, aliisque id genus conditionibus fœderis ageretur, mitti sane possit, qui nostro nomine statueret; suscipere autem in nos ipsos directionem tanti belli conjunctam tot tantisque cum periculis oneribusque et nostris et Regni nostri, a qua non tantum salus, sed quod omnium est maximum, fama ac reputatio nostra dependet, multo majus est negotium, quam quod concludi absentibus nobis possit aut debeat. Hæc in causa fuere, quod Legatum, qui nostro nomine statueret, Hagam Comitis non miserimus, tibique ea voluerimus significare, ut justo loco ac tempore nos excuses, ne id nobis a ceteris vertatur vitio : ac ne quod a nobis negligatur, quod facere quidquam possit, vel ad restituendam conservandamque causam communem, vel ad cœteros animandos, volumus ut tu ipse, cui meus voluntasque nostra notissima est, te Hagam Comitis quantocyus conferas, atque illic adjuncto tibi ordinario nostro Residente Rutgersio, legatis amicorum ac confœderatorum, quibus nostra propositio placet, isthic convenientibus, mentem nostram uberius explices, et ut Dominos suos ad Legatos huc mittendos incitent, author sis ac persuadeas. De animo vero nostro ac consilio sic statue, ceterisque assevera.

Primo, nos in proposito nostro, suscipiendaque directione istius belli pro restitutione rerum communium constanter perseverare, ac tertiam onerum partem sustinere velle. Hoc enim et si nobis, regnoque nostro grave sit, tamen ne minus excrescens potentia statui nostro plus satis inimica, in vicinia nostra ac ad mare Balthicum pedem figat, ducti et hac status nostri ratione, et amicorum commiseratione, periculis hisce nos subjicere non dubitamus; suscipere vero in nos id periculi, nisi secundum Deum fulciremur, viribus nostris id vero magnæ esset temeritatis.

Secundo, poteris et hoc asseverare, cuncta quæ obtulimus parata fore apud nos quocunque die, modo nobis tempestive quid ceteri velint, sentiantque innotescat: Noster miles (ut ipse nosti) quocunque die cogi potest, et magna sui parte sub signis est, præsertim mercenarius. Classis in Balthico mari parata, et octo nostræ naves in portu Gothoburgensi: tormentis bellicis, ceterisque ammonitionum generibus nihil cum opus erit, deerit, et nos ipsi parati futuri sumus ut rem adgrediamur, quamprimum inter nos, et ceteros confœderatos convenerit.

Tertio, quamque rei bene conficiundæ ratio non parum in celeritate et præveniendis hostibus sita est, tum ita maturandum erit ut firma fœderis subsecuturique belli fundamenta prius jacta sint, utque incommodis quæ subsequi possunt, prius cautè prudenterque prospiciatur. Nec putandum est moram exigui temporis adeo noxiam esse, quin compensetur consilii maturitate. Hæc non ideo scribimus, quod lenta probemus consilia, sed quod cuncta rectè digesta cupiamus ac tum demum fortiter constanterque rem adgrediamur. Nos semper parati sumus, nec erit in nobis culpa moræ. Si ceteris res cordi est, cogant pecuniam atque illam deponant ut haberi nervi rerum gerendarum possint, cum de fœdere ejusque executione convenerit. Hæc en unica et sola ratio est maturandi negotii; Nihil ex nostra parte deerit, vel deliberati animi, vel rerum, quas promisimus.

APPENDIX. 95

Cuncta nunc dependent a ceteris amicis quorum interest, hoc non negligi. Illos statuere optamus quod sit è re sua, et quid conferre vel velint, vel possint. Ac primo quidem, si ceteris negotium hoc curæ erit, optamus ut se uniant ac conjungant, quo nobis pro certo constet, priusquam negotium id adgrediamur, quos simus adjutores, quos amicos, quos hostes habituri; deinde ut de conditionibus fœderis à nobis propositis, tibique ac traditis, deliberent; sique illæ placuerint, ut Legatos suos ad nos mittant, qui de omnibus nobiscum statuendi et concludendi potestatem plenam habeant, adversum quos ita nos declaraturi sumus, ut cunctis patere possit, studium nostrum inserviendi saluti amicorum ac publicæ. Denique si agitur res serio, conferat quisque confœderatorum suam partem quo tam in ære parato trimestris stipendii et arma militaria, aut horum loco 4^{ti} mensis stipendium, atque sumptus pro militis conscriptione requisitos, qui necessario sunt in antecessum dandi, omnemque pecuniam Amstelodami in Banco (ut vocant) deponant quantocyus sub nostro nomine, ut eam tollere cum opus fuerit, atque in militum conscriptionem sustentationemque conferre possimus, neve liberum cuique sit, sine nostro jussu illam vel totam vel ulla sui parte attingere. Quod attinet conditiones fœderis à nobis propositas, quas tu innuis mitigari debere, ne ceteri fœderati metuentes onerum pondus, se subtrahant, sane non diffitemur conditiones has graves ac præstitu difficiles esse. Verum si quis facile putat bello lacessere potentissimum Europæ Principem fulcitum viribus Hispanicis, stipatum tot Principum Germanicorum ac, ut uno verbo dicamus Ligæ Catholico Romanæ robore, tum connectere dissolutas scopas ac consolidare tot animos diversa sentientes; denique erepta tenoribus possessoribus suo quæque Domino reddere; Nos hanc illi gloriam ceteraque quæ illam comitari possunt commoda, non inviti concedemus. In conditionibus propositis, exiguam securitatis nostræ Regnique nostri rationem habuimus, atque id quidquid esse oneri prope modum totum in nos suscepimus. Minoribus autem viribus adgredi tantum negotium, temeritatis magis, quam consilii esse putamus ac forsan cadere posse in hominem privatum vel obnoxium alteri obsequio, vel alias rationes sui conservandi ignorantem. A nobis certè, quibus Regnum à deo potens atque amplum concessum est, quique nihil præter famam in pretio habemus procul abesse debebit. Certe quisquis res magnas adgressus fuerit, sine magnis viribus, magnisque sumptibus ductus forsan vana spe, ac cunctis in casum datis, falsum se deceptumque tandem intelliget. Illud quoque non minus considerandum venit in conditionibus nostris, quomodo certi portus, ubi miles nostri exponatur, ac classis nostra pro anchoris stet, nobis pateant, tam in Balthici, quam Germanici maris litore. Id enim nisi obtineatur, facile est æstimare, locum nobis non futurum, ubi exercitum formare, ac necessaria, quæ subvehi debent, asservare possimus. Hæc atque alia tu diligenter inculcabis Legatis confœderatorum, qui adventuri sunt, ut de omnibus tempestive et prudenter constituatur quo hoc negotium tantum non tædio magis malorum quæ nos præmunt, aut metuimus, vanaque spe, quam maturo consilio, firmoque proposito susceptum videatur. At si Legati Confœderatorum, qui ad nos missi fuerint, nobis bonis rationibus demonstraverint, hostem cum quo nobis res futura erit, infirmiorem esse, ac minoribus viribus cogi ac dejici posse possessione injustè arrepta, aut militem sumptibus minoribus conscribi, vel stipendiis minoribus sustentari posse, quam nos putamus certè in hisce omnibus et ceteris, quæ levare tam nostra onera, quam reliquorum fœderatorum queunt, faciles ac promptos nos exhibebimus. Tuum nunc erit, cuncta hæc dextre explicare, quæque suo loco, Principesque, quibus ista Confœderatio placet, eorumque Legatos certos reddere. Nos si tempestivè aliquod ac serio de hoc tanto negotio constitutum fuerit, ab ipsis, atque demum per Legatos ipsorum ad nos delatum, et nobiscum conclusum, quod spes nos maxima teneat, per Dei Gratiam ceteris juvantibus faventibusque in pristinum suum statum rem communem restituendi. Hisce te Deo commendamus. Dabantur in arce nostra Stockholmiensi die 13 Martii A° 1625.

GUSTAVUS ADOLPHUS.

Magnifico et Generoso sincerè nobis fideli apud Senerissimum Magnæ Britanniæ Regem Commissario nostro Jacobo Spensio de Wormston et Equiti Aurato.

(*Indorsed*) Copie de la Lettre du Roy de Suede a Mons. Spens, du 13 de Mars 1625.

INDEX.

Anstruther, Sir R., receives information from Roe, 68

Baltic, the, designs of Gustavus Adolphus in, 75
Bethlen Gabor, his alliance hoped for by Elizabeth, 2 ; offers to join Gustavus Adolphus, 3
Brandenburg, Elector of, his meeting with Gustavus Adolphus, 39 ; is in evil case, 40 ; negotiates with Sweden, 72

Charles I. continues to interfere diplomatically on the Continent, 1 ; negotiates with Spain, 5 ; his instructions to Roe, 10
Charnacé, Baron, his part in the Treaty between Sweden and Poland, 36, 42, 43, 50 ; his mission to Gustavus Adolphus, 72, 82
Christian IV., King of Denmark, his treaty with the Emperor, 29, 31, 32
Coloma, Don Carlos, preparations in England for the reception of, 54

Danzig, opening of negotiations at, 79, 81
Dohna, Baron of, his arrival at Danzig, 77, 81
Dorchester, Viscount, his foreign policy, 1

Elizabeth, titular Queen of Bohemia, her correspondence with Roe, 2

Frederick, titular King of Bohemia, sickness of, 76

Frederick Henry, Prince of Orange, listens to Roe's proposals, 2 ; objects to negotiate with Spain, 5 ; Roe's negotiation with, 30

Gustavus Adolphus, King of Sweden, sends Spens to England, 5 ; his reception of Roe, 36 ; his character, 49 ; prepares for war in Germany, 52, 57; proposals made to him by Wallenstein, 59; his plans narrated by Oxenstjerna, 60 ; his continued preparations for war, 68; his designs in the Baltic, 75; asks for help from England, 82; lands in Germany, 84; his instructions to Spens, 85; his letter to Spens. 92

Lübeck, Peace of, disliked at the Hague, 29

Morgan, Sir Charles, arrives at Enkhuisen, 33

Orange, Prince of, *see* Frederick Henry
Oxenstjerna, Axel, Chancellor of Sweden, negotiates with Roe, 47; is questioned by Roe about his master's plans, 58

Pillau, tolls at, 41
Pomerania, Duke of, negotiates with Sweden, 72

Roe, Sir T., on his return from Constantinople, presents a memoir to the Prince of Orange, 2; returns to England, 5; proposes to Charles to intervene in favour of Gustavus Adolphus,

6; sets out on his mission, 9; his instructions, 10; his speeches to the States-General, 21, 22; his conference with Schwarzenberg, 26; gives an account of his reception in Holland, 28; negotiates with the Prince of Orange, 30; and with the States-General, 31: arrives at Konisberg; negotiates between Sweden and Poland, 36, 39; believes the truce settled, 46 ; proposes to go to Warsaw, 48; his description of Gustavus Adolphus, 49; goes to Warsaw, 53; his account of the Polish kingdom, 55 ; asks Oxenstjerna for information on the Swedish plans, 58 ; takes leave of Oxenstjerna, 74

Rügen taken possession of by Swedish troops, 81

Sanderson, Mr., appointed resident in Sweden, 77

Schwarzenberg, Count of, his conference with Roe, 26

Spens, Sir James, comes to England on a mission from Gustavus Adolphus, 5 ; his instructions from Gustavus Adolphus, 85

States-General, The, Roe's speeches and propositions to, 22, 23 ; their reply to Roe, 25 ; their reception of Roe, 31

Sweden, States of, reported resistance of, 57

Vane, Sir Henry, sent on a mission to the Hague, 5 ; returns to England, 6 ; returns to the Hague, 53

Wallenstein opens negotiations with Gustavus Adolphus, 59

ERRATUM.

In page 86, line 3, for " yourself " read " himself."

www.ingramcontent.com/pod-product-compliance
Lightning Source LLC
Chambersburg PA
CBHW020156170426
43199CB00010B/1069